Centre-Forwards: The Great Ones

The 'Great Ones' Series

SOCCER : THE GREAT ONES

CRICKET : THE GREAT ONES

CRICKET : THE GREAT BOWLERS

CRICKET : THE GREAT ALL-ROUNDERS

CRICKET : THE GREAT CAPTAINS

LAWN TENNIS : THE GREAT ONES

GREAT WOMEN TENNIS PLAYERS

GOLF : THE GREAT ONES

RUGBY : THE GREAT ONES

RUGBY LEAGUE : THE GREAT ONES

SHOW JUMPING : THE GREAT ONES

14.

CENTRE-FORWARDS:
The Great Ones

LAURIE MUMFORD

PELHAM BOOKS

First published in Great Britain by
PELHAM BOOKS LTD
52 *Bedford Square*
London, W.C.1
1971

7207 0362 x

Set and printed in Great Britain by
Tonbridge Printers Ltd,
Peach Hall Works, Tonbridge, Kent
in Baskerville eleven on twelve point,
on paper supplied by P. F. Bingham Ltd,
and bound by James Burn at Esher, Surrey

Contents

ACKNOWLEDGEMENTS

The author's thanks are due to the following for the reproduction of the photographs indicated:

Associated Newspapers Ltd: 2–4, 6–8, 10–15.
Syndication International: 1.
Central Press Photos: 5, 9.

He is also happy to acknowledge the help received in the preparation of the book from Harry Treherne and his staff at the *Evening News*

Illustrations

Introduction

Centre-forwards are a vanishing breed. If that seems an exaggeration, the term, at least, is an anachronism. Mention it on the soccer terraces of the seventies and the chances are a bystander will mentally dub you a square and hasten to put you right.

'Look here, mate,' I can hear him saying. 'We don't call 'em centre-forwards now. We have strikers. Our team play a fluid formation, see.'

If he warms to his subject, as many do in a soccer crowd, there will follow an erudite treatise on 'the system' and how the 'scientific' approach pays off, if not in goals at least in results. Gone, it seems, are the bustling, dashing heroes who used to bulldoze their way through the middle and billow the net with rocket-like shots from 30 yards or more. Today's defences are too well organised to permit that.

In the time between the wars and for some years after, the W system of forward play was the one most frequently followed, with the centre-forward well up and lurking in the target area. The inside men stayed back, acting as the link between the half-backs and the wingers whose primary task was to outflank the backs and provide the openings for their leader.

The first nail in the coffin of this system was driven home by Herbert Chapman when, as manager of Arsenal, he instructed his centre-half, Herbie Roberts, to stick close to the opposing spearhead and forget about the attacking forays in which contemporary pivots liked to indulge.

So Roberts became known as a 'policeman,' and clamped

the shackles so firmly on rival centre-forwards that the third back game became almost universal in British soccer. Little attempt was made to counter this addition to the defensive screen, an addition that was permanent and not just there part of the time so that the centre-forward might still enjoy moments of freedom. The result was that in match after match the key duel was that fought between the centre-forward on one side and the centre-half on the other.

This form of football served for some 30 years until Manchester City confused everyone by instructing Don Revie to wear the number nine shirt. They turned the W formation inside out and conventional football planning went with it. The W plan became an M plan with Revie the creator rather than the taker of chances.

At Wembley in 1953 the mighty Magyars of Hungary demonstrated how static our soccer had become by thrashing England 6-3 and just to show that that was no fluke they won even more convincingly by 7–1 in Budapest the following year. They achieved it with Hidegkuti wearing the number nine shirt but playing in a withdrawn style and creating chances for such as Puskas. The time had come when shirt-numbers meant nothing as far as positions on the field were concerned.

The lesson was driven home by the exploits of that brilliant Argentinian, Alfredo di Stefano, who played for Real Madrid when the Spanish club came to regard the European Cup as their exclusive property, holding it for five years in succession from the time of its inception in 1956 to 1960.

Many critics regarded the displays of di Stefano as the ultimate in centre-forward play which has not been matched since. No third back system was proof against him for he was as elusive as a hare and had an uncanny flair not only for finding the open space where he could receive the ball in the clear but also creating room for his colleagues.

The great Spurs team of the early sixties – in 1961 they were the first club this century to achieve the Cup and League double – gained their success with an old-style centre-forward in Bobby Smith. Considering his broad and powerful frame, Smith was tremendously mobile but most of all he had tremendous courage and stamina.

Every game found Smith engaged in fierce tussles in the

penalty area. It was a physical challenge from which he never shrank. Sometimes he took a hammering from this bodily contact. Though neat enough in much of his footwork he was not as artistic as some of his contemporaries but he kept the opposition so busily employed that time and again that arch goal-poacher, Jimmy Greaves, drifted through.

Few of today's centre-forwards try to blast their way through the middle. Jeff Astle, of West Bromwich Albion, and Everton's Joe Royle are about the nearest to the old concept in the top flight. They like to play the ball off to better-placed colleagues so that when the return pass or centre comes the ball is forward and they are running in to meet it, rather than waiting for a service from the rear which involves facing their own goal and turning, usually with a defender at their backs, before they can make any progress.

England's failure in the World Cup in Chile in 1962 was the forerunner of many changes, not least the appointment of Sir Alf Ramsey as team manager in place of Walter Winterbottom. Not that Mr Winterbottom had a bad record, for England won 80 and drew 33 of the 140 games while he was in control with a goal average of nearly two to one.

Sir Alf's great advantage was that he was gradually allowed to mould a *team* rather than field eleven star individuals. Without the squad training to promote the essential understanding that he built up over the next three years England would never have been fitted for the World Cup triumph that came in 1966.

The plans devised by Sir Alf Ramsey have been seen and described many times. Their essence was mobility and close support. He had Bobby Charlton nominally at centre-forward but playing the now refined type of game that had originally been tried by Hidegkuti and Revie. Charlton circulated in midfield, ever ready to pounce on any loose ball. Sometimes he would unleash one of the long thunderbolts for which he became renowned, but more often he probed as the inside men, those in the number eight and number ten shirts, raced forward, seeking out a goal passage.

This obviously had to have its counter, so teams evolved a double centre-half plan, willingly surrendering space in midfield so that they could keep control in the penalty area. The result inevitably was a crowded box and a further refinement in centre-forward tactics – the target player.

His role is to stand in the heart of the opposing defence, with his back to goal if necessary, and as the ball is sent to him from whatever angle flick aside to an onrushing colleague. Sometimes the move will be involuntary; it will just bounce off his foot.

In this situation the centre-forward acts as a wall almost. Only a rapid exchange of passes can defeat the present day close marking, so the aim is to create a triangle with the defender left stranded in its confines.

Defensive play has so developed that it is nine years since a First Division club scored a century of goals in a season. Reverting to the old-style centre-forward would demand a return to the old-style wingers capable of outflanking the rival backs. But with so much at stake not only in points and cash but in the exciting and broader horizons that success now brings to the elite, clubs cannot be blamed for making a barndoor defence their first objective.

Brazil proved in the World Cup in Mexico that an adventurous policy can still work, providing there are men like Pele to depend upon. Their defence was not as tightly-knit as some but there was so much flair up front that they always appeared capable of scoring more goals than they were likely to concede.

Some of their close work on the edge of the penalty area was reminiscent of the early days of football when the centre-forward advanced on goal with a posse of players round him like a battleship protected by destroyers.

Every World Cup has taught new lessons and promoted fresh thinking. Like fashion, soccer must ring the changes. Too many keen brains are at work in the background to allow it to stand still.

And it could be that in the not too distant future the centre-forward will be recognisable as such again.

I

Dean - the man who hated Dixie: George Camsell

William Ralph Dean wrote a little note: 'Have a good sleep; I shall be around tomorrow.' Then he folded it over a small bottle of aspirin, packed it carefully and posted it. The recipient was that great Liverpool goalkeeper, Elisha Scott, one of Dean's best soccer pals against whom he always reckoned to score a goal or two. It was Dean's little joke before every Everton and Liverpool derby game.

As the pair met on the pitch before one game Dean told him 'I'm due for a hatful today'. The staunch reply from Scott was that he had no chance. Yet within nine minutes Dean had completed a hat-trick.

But Scott was not the only goalkeeper who looked forward to facing Dean with some foreboding. The record books are splattered with Dean's scoring feats and his name has become almost a legend in the annals of the game. Although more than three decades have passed since he last wore the blue shirt of Everton it is doubtful whether there is a soccer follower anywhere who has not thrilled to the stories of his feats, for he was a king among footballers, a man it was impossible to overlook.

See the teams run out on the field and Dean could be recognised instantly. He had the looks, the build and the carriage that made him stand out, not merely among ten other players but in a crowd, too.

It was not that Dean was particularly tall. But he moved like a born athlete and power seemed to radiate from every muscle and sinew. He was deep-chested, heavy jowled and with crisp, black curly hair.

His legs tapered down to the tops of his neatly-laced boots . . . the boots which he insisted must have the toecaps hammered soft. He disliked shorts with tight elastic and the jerseys which he reckoned were about five inches too long. It is one of soccer's minor mysteries that the two never seemed to part company.

Dean, the son of an engine driver, was born at Bebington, Cheshire in 1907 and by the time he was 17 he was playing centre-forward for Tranmere Rovers. It was there that a supporter dubbed him 'Dixie'. Dean detested the name but it caught on with the public so that it stayed with him throughout his career although friends and associates called him Bill.

In March 1925, Tranmere parted with Dean to Everton for £3,000 which may not sound much by today's inflated standards but was a big fee in those days. No one can deny that it was one of the best investments Everton have ever made, for during Dean's stay at Goodison Park the club won the Second and First Division championships and the F.A. Cup in successive seasons from 1931 to 1933.

Within little more than a year of joining Everton Dean was seriously injured in a motor-cycle crash in which he fractured his skull. 'You'll never play soccer again' said the doctors.

But they had reckoned without the incredible spirit and courage of the man. When he came out of hospital the first thing that Dean set out to do was to ride a motor-cycle again to restore his nerve. That accomplished, his next hurdle was to see whether he could head a ball. He worked up from a child's ball to a soft bladder and then a light football. On the day he returned to the League side the ground was wet and the ball heavy. Yet Dean met a hard centre to nod it home as fearlessly as he had ever done. Those who knew the background story of his fight for fitness could scarcely bear to watch as the ball came across and Dean shaped to meet it. In a flash – and what an exhilarating moment it was – they realised that the fight had been won and Dean was back.

Two years after his arrival at Goodison, Dean won the first of his 16 caps – ten against home sides and six against foreign opposition. This may seem a modest total for such a great player but at that time internationals were nowhere near as frequent as they are now and England's participation in the World Cup was still more than 20 years away.

England drew that game against Wales at Wrexham and

Dean was picked for the big clash against the Scots at Hampden Park where the home side had proved invincible for 23 years. Dean was sitting in his hotel before the game when a man, who turned out to be a valet, approached him with a message from his master that he would offer ten pounds to every player if England won, and a similar sum to the scorer of each goal. Considering that the match fee was only six pounds this was a fabulous offer. Dean scored both goals in England's 2–1 win and pocketed £30 from the man who had seen every Scottish victory in the previous 23 years and couldn't bear the thought of them winning yet again. For a player of 20, as Dean was then, it seemed like a fortune.

The season that was to confirm Dean as soccer's super marksman lay ahead. In 1927, George Camsell, of Middlesbrough, who was Dean's great rival for the centre-forward berth in the England team, had smashed all League scoring records by notching 59 goals in 37 games. Altogether he had the ball in the net 75 times. 'Unbeatable' said the experts but Dean was soon to prove them wrong, though with three games to play he was still nine goals short of his target.

Incredibly this had been reduced to three by the time Everton took the field at Goodison Park, for the last match against Arsenal, the club against whom Dean had made his debut for the Merseysiders.

Everton had already won the First Division championship for the first time since 1915 so, as far as the 50,000 crowd who packed the terraces that day were concerned, the result was of secondary importance. Even so the atmosphere was electric and the tension showed as the Everton players bustled and hustled in their efforts to put Dean clear.

Thrills came from the start. The Everton goalkeeper fumbled to give Arsenal an early lead but within two minutes Dean had soared to meet a corner and with a deft flick nodded the ball into the net. Minutes more and Dean was clumsily tackled as he was going through. There could be no two opinions on who should take the penalty.

As Dean placed the ball meticulously on the spot one could have heard the drop of the proverbial pin. So the roar which greeted his rocket shot as it seared into the net seemed all the greater in contrast. Now Dean had equalled the record and there was time enough for him to score the third goal. The crowd relaxed, content to enjoy the soccer feast that was being laid before them but when half-time came the only further score was a goal to Arsenal which put them level.

Everton decided when they came out for the second half that they must end the suspense as quickly as they could. They stepped up the pace and swarmed into the Arsenal penalty area but defenders surrounded Dean so that time and again the passes intended for him were intercepted. On the few occasions he did get the ball he was tackled in a flash, thus denying him a clear chance. As the minutes ticked by it seemed that nothing short of a near miracle would break the deadlock.

The ground was fairly crackling with excitement as Dean prowled and probed, this man with the build of a Bruce Woodcock and the speed of Derek Ibbotson. Inexorably the minutes ticked away and then with just three left, it happened. Over came the ball from the left and as it soared into the Arsenal penalty area there was Dean poised like a coiled spring. He timed that jump perfectly, caught the ball squarely on the centre of his forehead and with all the strength he could summon from those powerful neck muscles nodded it emphatically into the goal. Goodison erupted.

As the roar of the crowd echoed round the ground, Dean made for the dressing rooms. 'Where are you going?' asked the ref. 'Off', replied Bill. 'I don't blame you!' was the official's rejoinder.

But that was just one of Dean's little quips and he was back in his place on the circle by the time the Arsenal men had the ball on the spot ready for the restart. True, the Londoners forced a draw but that was of little account; the record was his. It is one that has stood to this day and is unlikely to be broken.

By now Dean's fame had spread far beyond the shores of Britain and that same year he was offered £25 a week, which must have seemed a fortune, to go to America and play for New York Giants. Others to whom a similar approach was made rose to the bait but the idea did not appeal to Dean. His refusal came as a great relief to Everton for, as the Football Association had no jurisdiction over American clubs, they risked losing their star without receiving any fee in return. Some time later there were reports that Dean had been invited to go to Madrid but these were denied by the club.

The hat-trick against Arsenal brought his trebles that season to seven. Five more came the following campaign and though he was restricted to one in 1929-30 he bounced back with four more in 1930-31. On three occasions – against Manchester United, Sheffield Wednesday and Chelsea – he netted five times in a match. The last time was against Chelsea when he rammed home four in the first 23 minutes and had completed his nap hand by half-time.

It was in 1931 that Dean proposed and was accepted by a 20-year-old Liverpool girl, Ethel Fossard. They decided to marry in July and Dean was determined that there would be as little fuss as possible. In fact, he was so intent on keeping the ceremony secret that even the guests were not informed of the name of the church, being requested to assemble at the bride's home.

Unfortunately for Dean, the secret leaked out the previous evening and what made matters worse was that when he arrived at the church he found the doors shut, as another service was still in progress. As he waited outside for ten minutes passers-by were quick to recognise the Everton hero so that when the time came he was virtually swept into the church by excited spectators. When he and his bride emerged, women struggled with each other to greet them and police had to rescue the couple from the besieging mob so that they could reach their car.

But if Dean took a buffeting then, he took it on the field, too. He suffered an ankle injury which required an operation to remove two small pieces of bone and later came the removal of a cartilage from his left knee. He was used to being shoved in the back and having his shirt tugged. He once recalled in an interview how on one occasion when the ball was coming to him the rival centre-half whispered 'You won't get this one, Dixie.' So Dixie turned and held him, as he had been, and said 'And nor will you!'

Commenting later on a much more recent game, Dean said 'The players of my day were not all little angels but at least they were never nasty or bad tempered.' As for Dean himself, he was far more sinned against than sinner. He was quite fearless in his approach, never shirking a tackle, but he was also scrupulously fair and was as zealous of the reputation he built up for sportsmanship as he was proud of his scoring deeds. Although he never earned more than eight pounds a week as a player with a two pounds win bonus he was able to say: 'I played at the right time. I enjoyed myself.'

By 1933, Dean had won a First and Second Division championship medal and a Cup-winner's medal, when Everton beat Manchester City 3–0 at Wembley, all in the space of five years, but the following year came the first sign that Everton regarded him as being past his peak with the announcement that they were on the look-out for a new leader.

They had reckoned without Dean's incredible resilience. Altogether he spent 13 years at Goodison and it was 1938 before he was transferred to Notts County. In the meantime he smashed Steve Bloomer's record of 352 League goals. It took Steve 23 seasons; Dean overhauled him in 14 and went on to 379, a figure that has since been topped by Arthur Rowley.

Dean, strangely, left Goodison without a trumpet fanfare. He had played 399 games for Everton in which he had scored 349 goals. Now Notts County had paid £3,000 for him – the same sum that Everton had given to Tranmere – and his departure was made in such a hurry that he had to borrow an overcoat for the trip.

It is doubtful whether County found him the investment they had hoped, for after nine games with them his contract was cancelled in January 1939 and it seemed that his playing days were at an end. That is what Dean thought, too, until an offer came from Sligo Rovers to help them in the League of Ireland and it was while with them that he won yet another medal, this time an Irish Cup winner's one. But, despite the medals and the caps, Dean's proudest possession is the first illuminated address ever given to a footballer. It was presented to him by the people of Birkenhead on his 21st birthday and recalls his 'good sportsmanship, brilliant play, unfailing tact and initiative as a leader.'

There were other sides to Dean of which the crowds heard little, the calls on his pocket and on his services, neither of which he ever begrudged.

There was the time he came to London to play baseball for Liverpool Caledonians and the time when he joined the Army and refused a job as a physical training instructor, serving instead in the Tank Regiment because he wanted to be one of the boys.

But perhaps the most heart-warming story of Dean, the one that shows the compassion and generosity of this man, came when he answered a call to go to a hospital where a 15-year-old boy had been bed-ridden by a spinal injury received in a football match 15 months previously. The boy showed Dean his medal – the one he had won when his side had achieved the school league title and he had scored the deciding goal. And Dean knelt by the bedside and showed him all his. That night a stricken boy slept happily, with signed photographs of his hero tucked under his pillow.

In February 1946, on his release from the Forces, Dean was granted possession of a public house in Chester where he settled down with his wife and three sons, none of whom was interested in football. All seemed set for a secure future but those injuries had left their legacy and his dreams evaporated in 1962 when his legs would not enable him to do the work and he had to give up the tenancy.

For a period times were hard until Everton's millionaire club chairman, John Moores, decided to arrange a testimonial match for him. Dean had never had one when he left the club and this tribute came to him 26 years later. But what a tribute it was!

More than 36,000 people turned up that April evening in 1964 to see the Englishmen of Everton and Liverpool do battle with the Scots attached to the two clubs. It was just another friendly but the fans rolled up in their thousands, the greying fathers who had seen him play and the sons to whom his name was a legend.

Dean kicked off. Just one kick and he was rewarded with £7,000. Strange indeed for a man who had been accustomed to driving himself to the limit for eight pounds a week. And Dean's voice was choking with emotion when he told reporters after the match: 'I have a great many happy memories from my playing days but nothing can compare with this. More than half these fans have never seen me play.'

So the memory of Dean lingers on while the man who was such an ornament to soccer keeps contact with the game by working quietly and happily with a pools organisation.

* * *

But mention centre-forwards on Teesside and the name all those steeped in soccer lore will put forward is 'Camsell'. They will utter it with the fierce pride that is essentially Middlesbrough where the spirit was always one of aggression and ruthlessness.

Like most of those who watched him at Ayresome Park, Camsell had a tough background. He was neither graceful nor delicate, but he satisfied the hard-to-please customers, satisfied them because his blistering animosity to opponents seemed to be the very embodiment of what the terrace fans thought about the establishment in those days of depression during the late twenties and early thirties. The workless in the crowd – and there were many – scraped up their shillings to watch Camsell, not merely to see him steamroller the opposition, which he did frequently enough, but literally to identify themselves with a kick against authority. Camsell could hammer the foe, recognisable foe in different coloured football strips. That at least was something tangible, something they could see and appreciate, and a brief but necessary relief from their own futile kicks against the anonymous 'those' who had reduced them to the breadline. They felt militant but powerless. Then they saw Camsell, who bored through the opposition like a power-drill and they cheered because here they could see an enemy being overthrown, an enemy beaten on level terms, unlike their near hopeless fight against the frustrations of squalor and poverty that they faced the rest of the week.

Yet Camsell was a late developer in the football sense. The product of a Durham mining village, he was an out-of-work miner when he joined in a kickabout with some pals. He had never played the game seriously but Durham City, then in the third division of the Football League, realised his possibilities and signed him at the age of 18.

Middlesbrough brought him to Ayresome Park in 1925 and were soon congratulating themselves on their purchase for Camsell was their top scorer for nine successive seasons. He was not pretty to watch. His elbows would work like pistons and his bottom would protrude into the opposing centre-half. Short and stocky, he was the symbol of strength. He was deceivingly swift and his control was such that, once with the ball at his feet, he was one of the most difficult players to shake off it. Add to this a sure shot and an uncanny positional sense and it will readily be appreciated why Camsell was as much feared by second division rivals as Dean was in the first.

It is true that his record 59 League goals in the 1926-27 season was beaten by Dean the following year but it has never been bettered in the second division, or any of the other lower divisions for that matter.

And Camsell's scoring feats lifted Middlesbrough into the top bracket themselves in 1929. It did something more; it brought him the first of his nine caps and Ayresome fans will contend that there should have been more, and that often the preference for Dean was sheer prejudice. The prowling Camsell would spend a considerable time facing his own goal but when the ball came he could trap it and turn so quickly that frequently the opposing centre-half was left stranded. Often a pivot towered over him, yet there was nothing George liked better than the long high pass, so adept was he at bringing it down either with his head or his chest. If soccer needed a Houdini to escape the padlock effect of the policeman centre-half then Camsell was the ideal man.

Camsell became synonymous with Ayresome. Here was a shooting star and yet a static one. The ups and downs of the transfer trail were not for him.

When the time came to hang up his boots he stayed with the club, first as coach, then as chief scout and finally as assistant secretary. Never was a club blessed with a more loyal servant and he retired on pension after 38 years service in 1963, this great leader they had bought for a mere £800.

But Camsell was only 63 when he died in March 1966, fittingly within 50 yards of the ground which had been the stage for so many of his gritty deeds.

2

Lawton - The man who bought himself

Soccer's conveyor belt moves more swiftly than most. Youngsters with their sights on the stars step on gladly at one end to be jogged and jolted along until they are tipped in the box marked 'Reject' at the other. The journey is a rough one and many do not reach the end of the line. There are diversions along the way, some lucrative, others just a by-pass to that reject box where the landings are now softer but from where salvage is still a matter of luck.

When a star begins to lose his lustre, that is the time to dip into talent's milky way. If the ace flutters precariously at the top of the house of cards then reinforcement is necessary before the whole edifice falls flat.

Everton knew that some day, somehow, they would have to find a replacement for Dixie Dean. It was not so much a question of 'who would it be?' but 'who could it be?' Tommy Lawton provided the answer. In snapping him up the Goodison Park club showed greater perception than those responsible for picking the England schools' side, for though Tommy played in three schools' international trials and scored a hat-trick in the first he had to wait four years for a cap and then it came in the highest class.

In three seasons as centre-forward for Folds Hill Central School, Bolton, Lawton scored 570 goals and at eleven he was playing in the Bolton Schools' team with lads three and four years his senior. And yet his left foot was 'suspect'. Tell that to the top goalkeepers on the receiving end of this potent weapon in later seasons and they would give a look of incredulous disbelief. The fact is that Tommy worked for hours with a gym shoe on his right foot while he hammered away with a football boot on his left. He shot like a mule and when it came to heading he rose to the ball as easily as if he were climbing a ladder.

Since Tommy was brought up in Bolton, and it was at the Wanderers ground that he spent two evenings a week training, it seemed that Burnden Park would provide his gateway to big soccer. The rush for his services began after he had notched a hat-trick for Rossendale United in the Lancashire Combination but he was still 18 months short of the time when he could sign professional forms.

That meant he wanted a job, and openings weren't easy to find in Lancashire in the days following the big depression of the early thirties. Bolton offered him two choices. A butcher's boy for 7s. 6d. a week or a clerk at half a crown more. If Lawton had been left to himself he might have said 'yes' but behind him was his grandfather, James Hugh Riley, a blunt, tough miner, who needed no telling that he had a prize asset in his control. Riley did more than find Tommy a 50s. a week job working as 'assistant secretary' in the Burnley office, he negotiated a position for himself on the groundstaff as well.

In March 1936, Burnley were fighting to avoid relegation from the Second Division. Nothing could be lost it seemed by drafting Lawton into the side and so, at 16½ he became the youngest centre-forward to play League football. Lawton did not score that day but he kept his place and his five goals in seven games helped his club to avoid the drop.

Just four days after his 17th birthday and within hours of signing the necessary forms, Lawton signalled his entry into the professional ranks with a glittering hat-trick against Spurs when the man marking him was no less a figure than Arthur Rowe, who had already played for England.

'Go out and play your ordinary game' had been the seasoned advice from the dressing room. Simple? No, not when nerves are twanging at the midriff.

The whistle, and the game was on. Lawton had barely taken up his frontal station when the ball came through to him and, looking up, he saw a gap through the middle. Tommy streaked towards the goal and then shot with all his power, strength born through hours of dedicated training, often on his own. There was no stopping that drive, nor the header soon afterwards from a swerving corner that punctured the Spurs' defence.

Lawton was excited, too excited. He fluffed two simple

chances before pouncing on a far more difficult one to clinch his treble in the second half.

Three months later Burnley were ready to cash in on the youngster that had cost them a £10 signing-on-fee, and on the opening day of 1937 Lawton went to Everton while £6,500 changed hands – a record then for a player under 21.

Recalling the day he arrived in Liverpool, Lawton says: 'I asked a tram conductor the way to the ground and when he recognised me he said "you'll never be as good as Dean".'

Dean was Everton captain at that time and Lawton played about ten games alongside him at inside-right. There can be no conclusive answer as to who was the greatest. Lawton of the sleek dark hair was the taller – even at 16 he had been touching 6ft and scaling 12st. 12lb. – and there was no finer sight in soccer than to see him majestically striding on to a through ball but, brilliant header that he was, he once admitted that he could not equal Dean's power.

Three defeats at the start of the 1937/8 campaign heralded the big switch. Lawton was entrusted with the leadership of the attack and out went Dean, who had only one more game for the first team in mid-season when Tommy was injured. Casualties so plagued Everton that term that they had a relegation fight on their hands, but despite this Lawton totted up 28 goals which put him top of the Division One marksmen.

From relegation candidates one year, Everton zoomed to the League championship the next. That's how soccer fortunes escalate. From backs to forwards the side moved the ball with slide-rule precision, and Lawton was the man in the van delivering the goods.

Everton kicked off with six successive wins and in September Lawton gained his first honour – selection to lead the Football League forwards against the League of Ireland. On a wild September evening in Belfast, with rain so heavy and persistent that in the second half the game was held up while there was a concerted rush for cover from those on the unsheltered terraces, the Football League scored eight times. And Lawton's share was four.

Recognition by England was now only a matter of time and it came 16 days after Lawton's nineteenth birthday. He was one of three Everton players engaged in the match against Wales at

Cardiff and the centre-half opposing him was his own clubmate, Tom Jones.

Lawton admitted ruefully afterwards that Jones virtually blotted him out but Jones was powerless to intervene when he cracked home a penalty. Although England lost 4–2, Lawton kept his place in the side to meet the Rest of Europe in a match to commemorate the 75th anniversary of the F.A., and again he scored in a 3–0 win.

After November, there were no further international engagements until the following April when Lawton achieved the first of his three great soccer ambitions – to play against the Scots at Hampden Park. His second was to captain England, an honour which came to him just after the war when he became the first centre-forward to do so since Vivian Woodward in the first decade of this century. But his third, to play in a Cup Final at Wembley, always eluded him.

Not for 12 years had England won in the great bowl at Hampden Park where the famed roar is an awe-inspiring sound to the visitor experiencing it for the first time. With more than 100,000 fanatical Scots bellowing their encouragement, the noise swelled to a deafening crescendo as Dougal shot the home side into the lead, a lead they held until 20 minutes from the end.

Pat Beasley equalised and now it was a question of which of those stout defences would crack. As the minutes ticked away the answer seemed to be neither. The referee was looking at his watch when Len Goulden put Stanley Matthews away. That great winger cut inside, then veered outside, taking the ball and Scotland defenders with him towards the corner flag.

Lawton, whose anticipation in spotting a likely opening was one of his greatest assets hared towards the goal as Matthews centred before a defender could make an effective challenge. It was a great cross, devastating in its pinpoint accuracy, and before Dawson, Scotland's vainly groping goalkeeper, could pluck it from the air, Lawton, timing his leap to perfection, had nodded it firmly into the net. Of all the goals Lawton scored none was as priceless or dramatic as this although there were several that came close to it.

League clubs had fulfilled only three fixtures when the outbreak of war ended the planned programme in 1939. Everton had drawn twice and won once, Lawton scoring all their five goals, a crazy record for one player to be responsible for all his side's goals in a season!

Five years is a long time for a soccer player whose career expectancy, except in rare cases, does not extend far past the mid-thirties, and but for the hostilities there is no doubt that there would have been many more glittering landmarks in Lawton's career. As it was, he joined the Army and was kept in this country, playing in numerous matches for charity under all kinds of titles.

The great Lawton played for 30s a match with no win bonus at the end of it, and no contract, as all these had been suspended. In official circles he and his kind were regarded as among the great morale-boosters, entertainers whose artistry in whatever medium served, however fleetingly, to thrust the grimness of war into the background.

In January 1945, Lawton scored his 400th goal in senior soccer, a target he had taken only eight years to reach, but now things did not go so well for him. His wife, Rosaleen, had been in poor health and had been advised to move south. This worry so preyed on Lawton that he lost his form and his England place. During the summer, he put in a transfer request and though this was withdrawn he renewed it four months later. Naturally Everton were not keen to part. They had had only three years pre-war service from Lawton and they knew that with the resources of clubs drained throughout the country they could not hope to obtain a fee for him that was commensurate with his stature. And what is more, he had still to be demobilised from the Army.

In the circumstances, the reported fee of £10,500 that Chelsea paid for him that November was a tremendous sum but it fell well short of the record £14,500 that Arsenal had splashed out for the Welsh wizard, Bryn Jones, in 1938.

Lawton arrived at Stamford Bridge in time to play against Moscow Dynamo – the only time he played against Russians – in a match which was the curtain-raiser to what was at that time a novel tour. It ended in a 3–3 draw and, almost inevitably, Lawton was among the scorers. But it seemed that his most sensational scoring feats were to be reserved for the big occasion. He had notched four when England had crushed the Scots

8–0 in a wartime international, demoralised Belgium with a goal in 12 seconds and took only a second longer to score against Portugal.

Many believe now that that was Lawton at his peak. He had regained his place in an England side that had just been humbled 1–0 by the Swiss and had travelled on to Lisbon to face Portugal who were reputed to be the finest Latin side in the world.

Lawton's header crushed the Portuguese invincibility tag right at the outset and he went on to score four in a 10–0 triumph. This should have been the preface to another success saga but on his return from that tour Lawton went down with food poisoning, an illness which strained the relationship between himself and his club. Chelsea wanted him to go on a club tour to Sweden and their doctor ruled him fit to travel, but this view was not shared by his own medical adviser. In the end a specialist ruled that he needed to rest for some weeks but Lawton's outspoken comments on this, and several other matters such as expenses, did not endear himself to some of the Chelsea officials, and the 1947 season was not very far advanced when his request for a transfer was granted.

The day after he had been selected for his eleventh successive international, Chelsea picked him for their reserves as they did not want to use a player in their first team who had requested a move.

Of all the clubs that sought Lawton's services he finally decided on Notts County, being the first star to move from a first to a third division club while still at the height of his fame. Of that there can be no dispute for Lawton held his England place another 18 months. Why did he take what must have seemed to many such an appalling risk? The answer is that Lawton thought he was safeguarding his future for he was to have a supplementary job as a typewriter salesman.

So Lawton went to Meadow Lane in November 1947 and such was his magnetism that the average gate there rocketed from 9,000 to 35,000.

Lawton did not remain a Third Division player for long as it took him less than three years to drive the side to promotion, though by now he was more a maker than taker of chances. His guidance and shrewd distribution made a star of Jackie

Sewell who became soccer's most expensive player when he was sold to Sheffield Wednesday for £34,500 in March, 1951.

For five years County and Lawton were happy but then resentment crept in among the players at the preferential treatment they thought Tommy was getting while Lawton himself was tipped off that if the club clinched a deal for another centre-forward he would be out of the side. Lawton also fell out with manager Eric Houghton whom, ironically, he had recommended for the post when he himself had been offered the chance to become player-manager.

That post came to him within months of returning to London in 1952 and the man who signed him, Jackie Gibbons, little realised that he was taking on his own replacement. Such is the harsh reality of the soccer world with clubs chasing not only success today and tomorrow but always. The experience of being manager at Brentford served Lawton well but he could not combine that job and playing as well up to the standards that he set himself.

At 33, Lawton himself thought he had seen the end of active service in First Division football so it was as much a surprise to him as it was to the soccer world in general when Tom Whittaker, the then manager of Arsenal, asked him to go to Highbury and immediately drafted him into the side.

Arsenal needed a man like Lawton to put some bite into their attack yet in his first five months at Highbury his only goal was scored against Aston Villa and that was rubbed out of the records because fog caused the match to be abandoned.

Three years Lawton spent at Highbury and when he left to become player-manager of Kettering Town, in the Southern League in February 1956 it seemed that he was a spent force. Kettering added a modest £1,000 to the £62,000 that five clubs had paid for his money-making skill and glamour during his 20 years of League football, and the Northamptonshire club quickly cashed in on their investment. Lawton's first appearance in his new colours doubled the gate to 4,000 at a time when there was snow on the ground. That number would have looked lost on some of the vast stadiums that had provided a stage for Lawton's magic but to the locals it seemed phenomenal.

In just six months Lawton transformed the club into a high-spirited footballing family of three sides who between them scored 103 goals in 30 matches. It seemed that Lawton's goal flair was infectious and he had learned the secret of imparting his knowledge to others. By Christmas, Kettering were ten points clear of their rivals and they went on to become Southern League champions with a record 64 points.

Lawton's success did not go unnoticed outside, least of all by one of his old clubs, Notts County, who had slumped sadly from the prosperous days of Tommy's first stay there. Still, the offer they made to him of £2,250 a year and £250 expenses was too good to refuse and Lawton was as eager to tackle a challenge off the field as he was on it. Meanwhile Kettering retained his registration as a player and as Lawton had already drawn his Provident Fund money when he left Arsenal he was barred from playing League football anyway.

But Lawton had ideas of helping his struggling side in the Cup and set about trying to buy himself from Kettering. It took all Lawton's patience and persuasion in some protracted negotiations to whittle the fee for his own services down from £850 to £250.

By that time County's interest in the Cup had evaporated and when at last the FA granted Lawton a permit it restricted him to appearances in friendly games, one of which was to be at Kettering as part of the transfer deal.

Lawton's second stay at Notts County lasted only 14 months and was far from happy. His appointment had split the board of directors in a much-publicised and protracted wrangle and the internal troubles were reflected in lack-lustre displays on the field. Gates slumped to less than 13,000 and when the club plunged almost inevitably into the Third Division it was heavily in debt.

In July 1958, County took the generally prescribed step when a club is in trouble. They and their manager parted company. It is a wonder there are still candidates ready to take the game's hottest seats.

It seemed an easy step from headers under the bar to pints over them and for the next four years Tommy was mine host at a village inn outside Nottingham. But if some of the customers wanted their ale diluted with lemonade there was no weakening of Lawton's interest in soccer. For a period he was manager of

Kettering and a scout for Manchester City. He even returned to County yet again as a part-time coach.

Then County appointed him chief scout and Lawton gave up his job as a representative for a pools firm. But the end was the same. In came a new manager who wanted to do his own scouting.

So yet again Lawton was like his 23 England caps – on the shelf. He was there still when in July 1970 he was rushed to hospital with suspected thrombosis.

As Tommy sat recovering he said philosophically: 'I suppose I was born too early. Now there are guaranteed pensions and the rest.'

But many who will recall Lawton at his peak will wonder how many of the moderns will contribute as much to soccer's riches as did Lawton.

3
Gallacher and Milburn: Scots fireball and Tyneside terror

Of all the great Scots who crossed the border to meet and conquer the challenge of English League football none succeeded quite as dramatically as wee Hughie Gallacher. Yes, there was not much of him. He stood only 5ft. 5in. and his boots were size 6½. But they were two sticks of dynamite as far as opposing defences were concerned and when the ball was fastened on the end of one of them then opponents' alarm bells rang out loud and clear. Size made no difference to Hughie. Policemen centre-halves stood sentinel over him almost as if they were glued together and yet not infrequently when the moment of action came Hughie would hustle past them like a thoroughbred racing away from a carthorse.

On one occasion, Hughie, seemingly tired of the shadow that had hovered over him for three-quarters of the game, suddenly darted towards the corner flag although the ball was in play on the opposite side of the field. The centre-half, not to be deceived, followed him faithfully like a watchdog and in so doing left a yawning gap in the middle through which Gallacher's inside colleague gleefully raced to ram home the cross. Gallacher was yards away and his name did not appear among the scorers that day, yet it was his goal for all that. Perhaps it couldn't happen in these days of fluid defensive systems but, above all, Gallacher had much of what the modern game lacks – originality. He was a man of infinite flair, a virtuoso among centre-forwards.

It was once said of Gallacher that he wasn't born, he was quarried. His hometown was Bellshill, about ten miles from Glasgow, where the mine, the next pay day, and soccer were the dominant topics.

Our pits have produced more than coal through the years. They have provided Britain with a rich seam of athletes, for the tough life of the miner sharpens those essential characteristics of strength, courage and determination, which are so essential in the highly-competitive world of professional sport. On his way to work, Hughie would sometimes meet up with a pal and kick a stone or an empty can about. The friend was that little wizard, Alex James, whose skill as a linkman was one of the foundation stones of Arsenal's golden years when they swept to four League championships and three Cup Final appearances in the early 30s.

Some of the James magic in controlling a ball undoubtedly rubbed off on Hughie. Or perhaps it was the other way about. Whatever it was, Hughie's control was such that he was a most difficult man to dispossess. The way to play him was to shut off the supply line but that was never easy, for Hughie was quicker than most at spotting an opening and his positional flair was uncanny with the ball attracted to him as though he were a magnet.

His first serious soccer was with Bellshill who strangely played him at centre-half before moving him up into the attack, first at inside-right and then centre-forward. There Hughie stuck. No other position would do. He regarded himself as *the* centre-forward and, to be fair, many good judges of the time agreed with him. Half-hearted attempts were made during his career to switch him to the wing but Hughie invariably gravitated to the middle which he regarded as his rightful place.

Airdrie quickly profited from Gallacher's natural talents for he was their leading scorer in each of the four completed seasons he was with them before, in return for his services, Newcastle lined the Scottish club's coffers to the extent of the then fantastic fee of £6,500.

That it did not raise too many eyebrows was due to Gallacher already being a conquering hero. He had made his international debut against Ireland in 1924 and the following season played in all the home series so that he had become virtually an automatic choice. Little more than a month before his move to Tyneside he scored five goals in succession for the Scottish League against the Irish League and he treated himself to another nap hand off the luckless Irish when Scotland won 7–3 four years later.

But the limelight did not always shine clear and bright on Hughie. He was, like many great entertainers, an extrovert, either bemusing opponents by his sheer artistry or riling them with his tantrums. Gallacher's was a stormy passage. He had a fiery temperament and sometimes the taunts of opponents would have an effect on him similar to putting a match to a drum of petrol.

The buffeting he could take. Every game was a war to Hughie and he would frequently retire with the marks of battle all too plain to see – his legs, ankles and even his back were black and blue and his shirt torn. As his career developed and he lost that yard of speed and times he was laid off through injury lengthened, the bruises multiplied and the recuperative powers declined. But what annoyed Hughie were the taunts, for his domestic life was no bed of roses either. He married first at the age of 17 and was already separated, paying 25s a week maintenance, by the time he moved to Newcastle.

Tyneside dubbed him the 'Mighty Atom', a nickname which he earned by scoring 36 goals in piloting Newcastle to the League championship in 1926–27. In his first game for his new club just 12 days before Christmas he helped himself to an early present with two goals against Everton.

Even so, trouble and Gallacher seemed inseparable companions and at the start of the 1929 season, after having been suspended for two months and later reprimanded and warned about his future conduct, he asked for a transfer.

Newcastle were not eager to part with their fireball and the reason why became obvious when the following April, true to the fickle fortunes of the game, they were struggling against the threat of relegation. The board gave permission for him to lead Scotland's attack against England at Wembley where, two years earlier, he had shared in the 5–1 triumph of the immortal 'Blue Devils', but Gallacher, realising the plight of his club, opted to help them instead. It was a typically loyal and generous gesture as Hughie had missed only two internationals in six years. But it was one that paid off. Newcastle beat West Ham 1–0 and the club were safe.

The success and the sacrifice did nothing to weaken Hughie's determination to move. In 174 League and Cup games he had scored 142 goals for the Tynesiders but he was not destined to kick another ball for them. In May, Chelsea matched Newcastle's demand for £10,000 which, at that time, was twice as much as they had paid for any other player. So Gallacher came to Stamford Bridge where he joined a wealth of Scottish forward talent with Alec Jackson, Alec Cheyne and Andy Wilson in the attack.

Perhaps the mixture was too rich as the chief honours continued to elude Chelsea. Nor did Hughie like that £10,000 price tag. He was one of the first to experience the cramping effects of a huge fee on his shoulders. He complained bitterly – and Hughie was never silent on such matters – that his ability made him a marked man – and that referees tended to ignore the buffetings he took from the big 'uns while being quick to punish him when he showed any signs of retaliation, if only with his tongue, which was most frequently the case.

The bright lights of London did not dazzle Hughie for long, nor did the air of the south. At least, that was the tactful excuse he made to a colleague who asked if he had ever regretted leaving the North and Hughie replied: 'I would go back there tomorrow if I could'. And yet in his own way this extraordinary hot-headed character was as loyal to Chelsea as he had been to Newcastle.*

When he was suspended for two months for using filthy language to the referee, following what he thought had been a bad foul on him by a Grimsby player in the last game of the Christmas programme of 1931, he said: 'I am not complaining for myself. I can take my medicine. But when I think of the club it is just rotten.

'If I had kicked a man on the field I would probably have escaped with a week or two. But swearing! If a man can't swear occasionally what can he do?

'Chelsea can lick anybody. They are the most harmonious club I have ever been connected with. But here we are at the toughest part of the season and I am out of it. The prospect of not being able to help them has cut me up badly.'

Temperamental and unpredictable. That was Hughie. A difficult character and yet one who could sound out the views of his playing contemporaries without finding a harsh word spoken

*His second match for Chelsea was at Newcastle where he drew a crowd of 68,586 which is still the record for St. James's Park.

against him. Yet he would carry petulance to the extreme if he heard one word which assailed his fierce pride. A word out of place on the field and he was all belligerence, a weakness that some of his more unscrupulous opponents were quick to turn to their own advantage.

Hughie's scrapes with authority, both on and off the field, provided a spate of publicity, much of which he did not seek or desire.

Within months of arriving at Chelsea there were reports that he had been the target of an offer from Gateshead and it is a fair reflection of the tact, understanding and the patience of the Stamford Bridge officials at that time that Gallacher was still with the club after two years.

Then he, and his great pal, fellow Scottish international, Tommy Law, were offered posts as player-coaches by Nîmes. France had just turned to professional football and Nîmes were prepared to pay the two men £18 a week which was more than twice the £8 maximum terms Chelsea had been able to offer for their re-signing. In addition there was to be a signing on fee of £60 plus bonuses for matches played, wins and special training allowances.

Confronted with this glittering spectacle it is not surprising that Gallacher and Law refused to re-sign for Chelsea who were greatly concerned by the development, especially as they looked like losing their two stars without any transfer fee in return. The affair threatened to have such serious repercussions for English football in general that the FA, through the then secretary, Sir Frederick Wall, intervened with the French FA but still negotiations proceeded until Law, a hard-headed businessman, insisted on £2,000 being deposited in a British bank. Nîmes could not raise that guarantee and the whole deal fell through.

Possibly it was indicative of their relief that Chelsea made Gallacher captain for the 1932-3 season. To some, the choice might have seemed extraordinary for a man who cannot be depended upon to control himself is not normally an ideal subject to put in charge of others – yet when Newcastle had taken a similar step they had won the championship and Chelsea needed more of Gallacher's fiery and dauntless spirit, providing always that it was channelled on the right course.

The experiment was still in its infancy when early in September Hughie received a groin injury which proved so troublesome that from then on his appearances were only intermittent. Even so, come August 1933 and he was again made skipper. Alas, by Christmas Chelsea had won only three games out of 18 and were floundering at the foot of the First Division.

Chelsea dropped their pilot and Everton promptly made an offer to him as they had Dixie Dean injured at the time. But Hughie stayed on at the Bridge, and even won back his place in the Scotland side that went down 3–0 to England at Wembley – Hughie's first cap since moving to London.

When the breach with Chelsea finally came, it was mainly through consideration for a third party – a Gateshead girl Hughie married in September 1934. She wanted to move north and when Derby paid a reputed £3,000 for him it was agreed that £200 should go to his creditors. His earlier protracted divorce proceedings had so drained his resources that a month after his second wedding he was declared bankrupt, a position from which he was discharged while at Derby.

Hughie was now 32 and past his peak but he was still good enough to win another cap, helping to avenge the defeat of the previous season when Scotland beat England 2–0 at Hampden Park. In eleven years Hughie had won 19 caps, no bad haul at a period when internationals were restricted to the home tournament, although only two, both against England, came between 1930 and 1935.

Gallacher trod a similar path to Dixie Dean and Tommy Lawton in that he, too, had a spell with Notts County before moving on to Grimsby and Gateshead where he finished his active playing career in 1938. In League football alone he had scored 386 times, exceeding even Dixie Dean's total by seven but falling 24 short of the total achieved by that other great Scots wizard, Jim McGrory, who notched 410 for Glasgow Celtic and was frequently Hughie's rival for the centre-forward spot in the national side.

Not for Hughie the rocky path of a soccer manager. Instead he settled down as a factory worker in Gateshead where he kept his interest in the game by watching Newcastle and playing in charity matches. He was still turning out when he was 50, often playing at inside-right to another great northern stalwart, George Camsell.

But now the crowds had gone, his second wife had died and his two elder sons were in the RAF. There remained his youngest son, Matthew, and Bill the budgie. Hughie was lonely and the bottle proved a false companion. That was the background to tragedy for on 28th May, 1957 Matthew was taken out of Hughie's care, taken away because he had struck the 14-year-old boy he idolised, with a metal ornament. Hughie did not know how it happened for he was drunk at the time. And so the law stepped in and the following 12th June he was due to appear at Gateshead Magistrates Court to answer charges of assault, ill-treatment and neglect.

June 12th never dawned for Hughie. At 11.30 the previous morning two grandchildren of the chairman of Gateshead, Hughie's last club, were train-spotting when they saw a man pace up and down a footbridge and then scramble down an embankment as the York to Edinburgh express thundered towards them. Minutes later a signalman reported that there was a body on the track. Hughie had come to the end of the line.

It was in that same month of June that Newcastle parted with the greatest centre-forward they had had since Gallacher. And, ironically, after waiting 14 years since Hughie's departure south to find a worthy successor they did not at first realise that their search had ended when they said "yes" to a written request from Jackie Milburn for a trial. For one thing he cost nothing and for another, when he signed direct from Army Training Corps football, he was developed as an outside-right. And Jackie agreed with that because he thought he would never be good enough in the air to make a centre-forward. But he had many other attributes which were to make him not only the idol of the North East but of England.

There were 73 Milburns in the village of Ashington where Jackie was born and whoever was responsible for giving him the initials J. E. T. must have been blessed with remarkable foresight for 'Wor Jackie', as he was known from Berwick to Middlesbrough all along the coast and rolling hills of Northumbria, was just about the fastest man ever to put on a number nine shirt.

Not unnaturally, coming from a great soccer family, the game was in Jackie's blood, but his education in it was, frankly, a hotchpotch. He never had a recognised junior club though once he scored 12 goals for Rec Rovers at Ashington when he was 15. With the ATC he scored 140 goals in two seasons. In schools soccer, such as East Northumberland Boys, who reached the semi-final of the English Schools' Shield while he was in the side, it made little difference to him whether he was left-back, centre-half or inside-left. After all, it was a game of soccer.

Newcastle at once recognised the incredible speed of this rangy youngster with the wide grin and the carefree spirit. The sheer momentum of that raking stride enabled him to outflank defences time and again, so it was a natural conclusion that he would serve Newcastle best on the wing.

Once later, while training with the England players, he won an unofficial sprint championship over 100 yards. His amazing power of acceleration would have made him a formidable rival on the track and it had been his ambition at one time to carry off the Powderhall professional sprint prize. That particular spur had its origins at Ashington, which was as renowned for producing runners as it is footballers. As an errand boy, Jackie would run all the way; he was the customers' favourite whenever anything was needed in a hurry. Perhaps they would have been surprised had they known that Jackie was not doing it merely out of consideration for them. They were just the beneficiaries of his own searing ambition to lower his best time from house to shop!

Milburn himself used to insist that Newcastle were a better side when he was on the wing, yet his most spectacular feats were achieved at centre-forward, for it was not merely his fleetness of foot that made him so dynamic. His control was such that he could 'glue' the ball to his toe with hardly any perceptible slackening in pace and he packed a deadly shot in either foot. In one experiment during his career, Milburn was timed kicking a dead ball over a distance of 48 feet. The speed worked out at 53.7 mph. At that rate a penalty shot takes less than half a second to cover the 12 yards from the spot to the goal-line. The inference is obvious. If Milburn was in range and on target the goalkeeper had little chance short of the ball being drilled straight at him.

The Newcastle forward line was by no means a settled unit when Milburn entered League football and it was manager

George Martin who decided to play him at centre-forward against Bury. Jackie's response was to score three goals and, indeed, such was his impact that after 24 games he was awarded his first cap against Ireland at Belfast in October 1948.

But despite that breakthrough it was not a happy period for Milburn. For one thing, Newcastle had switched him to inside-left and Milburn, seeing this as a threat to his international career, requested a transfer on the grounds that if they could not play him at centre-forward would they find a club for him that would?

For another, his wife, Laura, whom he had married 18 months earlier, was expecting a baby and was not in the best of health. Jackie had met this pretty Glasgow blonde at Letchworth, for she had moved south with her parents who had set up home at Willesden Green. This all gave rise to considerable conjecture that Jackie would follow the example of Tommy Lawton who, three years earlier, had moved from Everton to Stamford Bridge on account of his wife's health.

Laura never watched Jackie play unless it was a really big match but as an engagement present she gave him a small ebony elephant which Jackie carried in his shorts as a good luck talisman.

That was not his only lucky mascot for, on the eve of the 1951 Cup Final, he received a very special penny from the daughter of Frank Watt, who had given a lifetime of service to the club as secretary and had died earlier in the season. The penny had been carried by Neil Harris, the centre-forward who scored the day Newcastle beat Aston Villa for the Cup in 1924, and again by Jack Allen, the leader of the attack eight years later, when his goal helped to take the trophy back to St. James's Park with a 2–1 win over Arsenal.

Perhaps a remarkable incident at the end of that eventful October helped to settle all doubts about Milburn's future. As Jackie unsuspectingly accepted the offer of a lift into town he was blindfolded and taken to the Newcastle Medical School where students tied him to a chair. The kidnappers then made a ransom demand to the club threatening that if a contribution was not made to their Rag Week Milburn would not be released in time for that afternoon's match.

The police were called in, a rendezvous was arranged with

the students at a shop, and after two hours captivity Milburn was released less than 90 minutes before the kick off. Though the club was naturally peeved at the trouble and worry the incident had caused them, Jackie brushed it aside with his customary good humour and it certainly had little effect on his play for he scored the only goal that beat Liverpool.

Although critics maintained that Milburn was apt to be too nervously taut to play at his best in representative matches, he was a fixture in the England side for the next home international tournament and he was picked for the match against Wales in October 1949. It seems that these two successive Octobers were fateful periods for Jackie as just previous to the big game he twisted a knee. He won his race for fitness but then in the match itself fell heavily and broke his right wrist. This injury banished him from the centre-forward berth for a time as Newcastle preferred to play him on the wing sooner than risk further damage.

In a later October, 1951, he played against France and then lost his place in the England side. Yet that was the year when Jackie, now 26, was at his peak and at the threshold of a golden era for himself and for his club, who won the Cup three times in five years.

Whether it was those lucky mascots or not nobody will ever know, but just whisper the word Cup to Milburn and he seemed to become inspired. Yet of the 22 players who trudged back to the dressing rooms after a goalless first half in the 1951 Cup Final there was no one more disappointed than Jackie.

Early in that encounter with Blackpool, Jackie had leapt with joy as one of his drives hurtled into the net. With his arms aloft he pivoted round to see the referee not pointing to the centre spot as he expected but signalling a free kick for Blackpool. The referee was certain Milburn had handled in bringing the ball under control; Jackie was equally convinced that he had done no such thing. Only his now limp posture revealed his inner feelings. Milburn was too much of a sportsman to indulge in any tantrums or remonstrate with the referee. He bore the surprised look of a boxer who, after hammering his opponent all round the ring, takes a haymaker on the chin. The trouble was Milburn's fear that those lucky charms, the ebony elephant and the penny, were not going to work. True, Laura was sitting in the stands and she had never seen Newcastle lose. But that didn't mean much because she now had two little daughters and rarely watched them anyway.

During that interval pep talk it was decided to make more use of the long pass to try to prise open the Blackpool defence. And the chance to do just that came within minutes of the resumption.

Milburn was only just over the halfway line when George Robledo pushed the ball to him. He glanced at the linesman to make sure he was onside, noted that the backs were wide and square, and hared through the gap as centre-half Eric Hayward tried vainly to intercept. The opening was so clear-cut that everyone in that vast Wembley Stadium could size up the situation, and the atmosphere was electric as the gap between the flying Milburn and the prancing goalkeeper, George Farm, narrowed. As Farm tried to narrow the angle, Milburn swerved and then with perfect judgment coolly stroked the ball wide of his right hand into the bottom corner of the net. This time there was no mistake as an exultant Milburn rushed back into the arms of his delighted colleagues.

Soon afterwards Milburn made certain that the Cup would go to Newcastle with another goal. This was a remarkable effort, explosive in its impact, and such a contrast to the first in execution that fans still argue to this day which was the better of the two. Ernie Taylor, later to help Blackpool win the Cup, backheeled to Milburn well outside the penalty area and towards the right wing, almost 30 yards from goal. Without a moment's hesitation Jackie crammed all the power of his muscular frame into a left-foot shot. The ball skimmed across the turf at such a pace that it streaked past the startled Farm before he could make any real move to save.

Of all the many thrills at Wembley, this must rank as one of the greatest and it was a little sixpenny ball that set things rolling. The ball was one of Milburn's most coveted possessions as a boy for with it he had laid the foundations for his craft and shooting power on top of a pit at Ashington.

But if that Final was a triumph for Milburn it was a sad blow for Stanley Matthews. That great wing wizard was desperate to crown his career with a gold medal and he put in more direct shots at goal in that game than he normally allowed himself in half a season for he was the maker rather than the taker of chances. Milburn's brilliance meant that Matthews' opportunity might have gone for all time but, in fact, just two years later he was the architect of that remarkable rally by Blackpool when they overhauled the Lofthouse-led Bolton.

The next year Milburn was at Wembley again when George Robledo scored the goal against Arsenal which kept the Cup on Tyneside – the first time at Wembley that a club had won the trophy twice in succession, a feat since equalled by Spurs in 1961 and 1962. During that summer Milburn went on a club tour of South Africa where he received a knee injury which required an operation. But he made such a complete recovery that his speed was unimpaired and Newcastle began to use him more on the wing.

It was Milburn's speed which proved such a decisive factor when Newcastle returned to Wembley for the third time in five years and overcame Manchester City by three goals to one. Jackie was almost 31 but still hailed as one of the fastest men in the game and he, more than anybody, had guided Newcastle to that last stage, never more so than in a three-game marathon tie with Nottingham Forest. In the first tie, it was Milburn who snatched the late equaliser to make a replay necessary; in the second, operating on the wing, he proved a constant menace; and in the third he made two of the goals, the decider coming just a minute or so from the end of extra time. In the gallery of great players who never let up, Jackie deserves a prominent place.

Milburn treated Wembley to another of his specials in that 1955 Final. Neither he nor his fans rated him highly as a header of the ball and yet there he was, in the first minute, soaring to a corner from Len White to nod the ball decisively wide of that great German goalkeeper, Bert Trautmann.

No climber can stop on top of the mountain indefinitely and during the following season Milburn's displays fell short of the high standard that he had set. His path as a centre-forward had been eased for him by having such players as Taylor, Len Shackleton, and George Hannah to scheme the openings but now Jackie was the forager while Vic Keeble took over the centre. Then he switched to the right wing and found himself looking for someone to pass to instead of streaking off on his own as he had done previously.

England had not capped him since the game against France in October 1951 and it is a measure of his tenacity that after four years he was recalled against Denmark in Copenhagen – as the wing replacement for Stanley Matthews – to provide a fitting climax for a fleet-footed player whose career had turned a full circle.

It was appropriate, too, that when he left Newcastle after 14 years during which he had made more than 350 League and 43 Cup appearances, he should sign for the Irish League club, Linfield, with the same pen that was used to begin his career at St James's Park. Why Linfield? There were several reasons for the move to Ireland. Primarily, Jackie thought that it would benefit Laura's health. Secondly, he was offered the highest salary ever paid at that time to a player in the Irish League. And thirdly, as player-coach, he saw this as the first stage of a five-year apprenticeship in football management.

Ironically, just after England had beaten Ireland 3–0 at Windsor Park, Belfast, Jackie went to the same ground and scored six, a feat which had the local scribes expressing the view that some means should be found of cloaking his origin so that he could be included in the national side. In two of the happiest years of his career Milburn cracked more than 100 goals so that in 1958 he was elected Ulster's Footballer of the Year.

Such was his resurgence that he hankered for a return to League football and such his popularity that he had 23 offers to join clubs in England and Scotland. Birmingham led the hunt but Jackie had drawn his Provident Fund money in order to send Laura to Canada for a holiday and it is an inflexible rule of the trustees that the withdrawal of this money automatically debars the recipient from playing League soccer again.

Instead, Jackie took his boots to Yiewsley,* boots which had been constant companions since his Newcastle days and were now held together by pink sticking plaster. He took them to a club whose sky-high aspirations were in keeping with their ground on the fringe of London Airport. And he made such a good job of it that when, in January 1963, Ipswich wanted a

*Now Hillingdon Borough.

new manager it was Milburn they chose in front of 60 other aspirants.

Years earlier, Milburn had said that he did not fancy a manager's chair, yet here he was with typical Geordie phlegm taking over one of the toughest seats possible – the one vacated by Alf Ramsey. Ipswich had achieved a near miracle by winning the League championship in 1962 but they were already on the slide by the time Jackie arrived. He could not halt it and in 1964 they were relegated after winning only 17 out of 65 matches while he was in control.

Ipswich did not make Milburn a scapegoat. Sad Jackie resigned. He reckoned that he had travelled 40,000 miles round Britain in his search for players and the worry of trying to produce a winning team on a shoestring budget had affected his health.

That is how Jackie bowed out as a football figure. Bowed out? He could not be parted from his loves for long. He returned to Newcastle where he became a soccer columnist and where his son works in an office. In his spare time Jackie still hits a ball with relish – with a golf club.

When I called on the family home at Benton, Jackie was out, almost inevitably at St James's Park. But Laura told me happily: 'This is a good spot for getting around and once a Geordie, always a Geordie, you know.'

'And has Jackie an active connection with the club still?' I asked.

'Well, I wouldn't like to say that he *does* anything but his name is on the Supporters' Club notepaper,' she replied with a twinkle.

And long may it remain there.

4
Lofthouse the Lionheart

Nat Lofthouse sat in his managerial office at Burnden Park and paused ruminatively when I asked if we would ever see another centre-forward like him. 'We have a young player up here now, Paul Fletcher,* who can run, head and shoot. Those qualities are absolutely essential. They will be just as necessary for the front runners of the future whatever you care to call them. No team can succeed without punch in the middle.'

Lofthouse could have added courage to the list of requirements for during his playing days for Bolton and England he was the very personification of it, a leader of swashbuckling skill with a heart as big as the goalmouth. Not for nothing was he called the Lion of Vienna.

It has frequently been said that Bolton is famous for three things – cotton, clogs and Nat Lofthouse – so let's take a look at this Lancashire native who played the game of his life and personified his whole career one Spring day in May 1952. It did not seem an ideal time to play an international where so much prestige was at stake, for only three weeks earlier the England players had finished the long and arduous home season and there were fears that their preparation might not have been sufficient to counter the running down, the inevitable reaction of a lay-off following months of supreme physical effort.

Vienna was a city of dreams, not this time of romanticism and the waltz, but of soccer conquest. Only the previous season Austria had drawn at Wembley and now they believed they had the finest team in Europe. Victory now, similar to the 3–2 triumph they had gained in their capital in 1936, would confirm their right to the unofficial championship of Europe. A week earlier, England had managed only a 1–1 draw against Italy in Florence and spying Austrian officials had seen nothing in that performance to dent their confidence.

England's task became even more daunting when one under-

* Since transferred to Burnley for £60,000.

stood the political tension which frequently comes to the surface in sporting fixtures played the wrong side of the iron curtain. This was no ordinary away game; it was a battle on foreign soil.

As the players reached the Prater Stadium in the Soviet sector of the city they noticed that it was ringed by armed Russian troops. And in the crowd were Russians, Germans, Swiss and Frenchmen, all relishing the prospect of the erstwhile soccer masters being humbled once again. There were also 2,000 British, mostly troops, who went to the stadium that wet Sunday afternoon with dark thoughts of the ridicule they would have to endure if England were beaten.

So it was a grimly determined squad that Billy Wright, the man of 105 caps, led out in front of that chanting crowd. And indeed it was Wright who was the hub of the defence while Lofthouse marshalled the forwards, probing, wandering and always seeking a chink in the Austrian armour.

Lofthouse found one and scored, Austria countered, fighting England went ahead again only to be pulled back once more as the Austrians swept down on their goal. It seemed that every yard of ground was to be bitterly disputed but as Wright and his defenders showed no signs of faltering so Austria's confidence began to melt. Anxiety took the place of arrogance. They began to make mistakes and missed the chances that their relentless pressure inevitably provided.

The crowd screamed with a grim, frightening intensity but with ten minutes to go the score was still 2–2. Austrian pride would not brook such a deadlock. They grouped themselves for a final assault and it seemed that no sooner had an England player made one bold interception or desperate clearance than he was called upon to make another.

Eight minutes left and still the Austrians had not beaten England goalkeeper, Gil Merrick, again. The Austrians forced a corner and up they surged as Melchior lashed the kick menacingly into the goalmouth. But there was Merrick leaping above the ruck to pull the ball down as surely as if he was plucking an apple off a tree. Merrick did not punt the ball out, but threw it so that it landed in front of Tom Finney.

The Austrians, fatally committed to all-out assault, were stranded. Only the left-back, Happel, stood between Finney,

Lofthouse and the Austrian goal. Finney with that ice-cool precision which was his hallmark and made him one of the greatest wingers ever to don an England shirt, craftily floated the ball beyond Happel's despairing lunge and there was Lofthouse off on his long thrilling journey.

Nat took only one route to goal on that trip – the shortest. Straight as a bullet he hared into the Austrian penalty area, his tongue clamped between his teeth which was one of those little unconscious mannerisms he always effected at moments of supreme effort and concentration. As Nat bore down on him, goalkeeper Musil seemed rooted to his line. When would he shoot? No, it seemed that nothing would stop the charge except the net itself. Ten yards, eight yards, six yards and then the goalkeeper, suddenly galvanised to frantic action, hurled himself at the Englishman.

A split second before the goalkeeper crashed into him Lofthouse slipped the ball forward. For an agonising moment as the two went down in a heap it looked as though the chance had gone. But Nat had released the ball at the crucial point and there was no one within yards who could prevent it rolling inexorably on and into the net to bring England a famous victory.

Nat they carried off on a stretcher as the cheers of the England contingent reverberated round that stadium, but such was the courage of this man that he insisted on returning for those last few dramatic minutes and though only hobbling on the wing he yet managed to crash a shot against a post before the final whistle.

Like Tommy Lawton, Lofthouse went to Castle Hill School, Bolton, where he decided he would like to be a goalkeeper. Well, it made a change from wanting to be a centre-forward which seemed to be the ambition of all his mates, fired as they were by Lawton's early successes. In any case, Nat did not have to look beyond his own family to find a rival for the leadership of the attack. He thought his brother, Tom, would do the job better. But his schoolmaster converted Tom to centre-half and thought Nat would do better up front.

For two seasons Lofthouse played for the Bolton boys team, once scoring seven goals in an 8–1 win, which earned him his first bicycle promised to him by a friend of the family if he achieved a hat-trick. Lawton had slipped through Bolton's hands but no such mistake was made by the Burnden Park club with his successor, who joined their groundstaff when he was 14 and 18 months later he scored two goals in his first senior game, against Bury. That was in wartime regional football, his League debut coming in the first post-war season when his 18 goals put him top of the club scoring list, a place he held for eleven of the next 13 seasons.

When Lofthouse began in League football there was not the opportunities for overseas trips that exist now but in 1950 he used a passport for the first time when he toured Canada with an F.A. team.

In one game Lofthouse kicked off 20 times and reckons they were the only kicks he had throughout the game. The opponents, Saskatoon, were two men short and Lofthouse was one of the players lent to them to make up the number. Poor Nat stood a lone, helpless figure up front as his colleagues gleefully rapped 19 goals past the Canadian goalkeeper. And that 20th kick? That was when Nat set the ball rolling at the start of the game!

Nat had already made the first of 15 appearances for the Football League when England, who had already tried six centre-forwards in their efforts to find a successor to Lawton, turned to him for the match against Yugoslavia at Highbury in November, 1950. He scored both goals in a 2–2 draw, was passed over for the game against Scotland at Wembley, but was recalled to make his first appearance at the stadium against Austria when he proved almost as big a thorn to his rivals as he was to prove in that memorable match the following May.

Lofthouse reckons that his first performance against the Austrians was one of the best of his life and in the 2–2 draw he scored a goal from a move worked out in his hotel room beforehand. The Austrians had a plan where the centre-half kicked a high ball across the field and over the back's head for the winger to run on to. Melchior, in fact, netted for them with this ploy and Alf Ramsey, then one of the England backs, thought he and Lofthouse could work a similar plan. Ramsey told Lofthouse to 'hide' himself at outside-left when a free kick came in a suitable position and he would endeavour to put the ball on his head. As it transpired, the opportunity that had been

DIXIE DEAN . . . 'He had the looks, the build and the carriage that made him stand out . . .'

GEORGE CAMSELL . . . 'his blistering animosity to opponents seemed to be the very embodiment of what the terrace fans thought about the establishment in those days of depression'

TOMMY LAWTON . . . 'there was no finer sight in soccer than to see him majestically striding on to a through ball'

envisaged duly arrived and Ramsey placed the kick with pin-point accuracy so that the unmarked Lofthouse could net easily.

Wembley always did something for Nat. He felt that if he could not play well there he could not play anywhere and he had two goals in each of his next two matches there against Wales and Belgium.

His next appearance there was to be one of the greatest soccer occasions of the decade, the Coronation year Cup Final of 1953 when Blackpool, losing 3–1 with only 25 minutes left, plucked a glorious 4–3 victory in what has gone down in history as 'Matthews' match'.

Inevitably, Lofthouse had done as much as anyone to put Bolton in their first Cup Final since their victory over Portsmouth 24 years earlier for he had scored in every round and was out to share the record which his opposite number, Stan Mortensen, had achieved for Blackpool in 1948. Lofthouse had to wait no longer than 90 seconds to achieve that mark, for his first shot, a powerful low drive from 25 yards, glanced off the arm of goalkeeper Farm and into the net.

Only 15 minutes had gone when Bolton were handicapped by an injury to their left-half Bell but that in no way blunted the thrust of Lofthouse who throughout was like a dagger poised at Blackpool's throat. Twenty minutes and Lofthouse was through again to lash a drive against a post with Farm stranded. When Hassall deflected a Mortensen shot into his own goal to put Blackpool on terms, Bolton immediately hit back through Moir and their lead looked unassailable ten minutes after the break when the limping Bell made it 3–1.

For the rest, Lofthouse was an unwilling spectator of the Matthews' magic as the great wing maestro taunted and then tore the Bolton defence to shreds. It was Matthews who made a goal for Mortensen and it was Matthews again who clinched it. With three minutes left, Mortensen had fired home a free kick as surely as shooting a bullet from a gun and then, with only seconds remaining, Matthews laid a chance for Perry on the proverbial plate.

Afterwards Lofthouse was one of the first to congratulate Matthews with: 'Bless you, Stan lad, it couldn't have happened to a better player.'

Lofthouse was voted Footballer of the Year in that same season when he played in all the home internationals, but five years were to pass before his next appearance in a Cup Final – one of the most poignant Wembley games of all time.

Three months had gone since the Munich air disaster, a crash in which eight leading Manchester United players had been killed, yet here was their patched-up team at Wembley for the second year in succession. In ten weeks since the crash United had fought out 14 League games and six F.A. Cup-ties, swept forward on a vast emotional tide. Outside Bolton it seemed that the whole sporting world was willing United to the Cup triumph that had eluded them when they met Aston Villa 12 months previously.

As the teams emerged from the tunnel, Lofthouse as captain, led them but previously he had preferred to be last but one in the Bolton file. Most players have their little fads and superstitions and this was one that Lofthouse owned up to because it made him feel more at ease. Only he and Doug Holden remained of the side that had gone down to Blackpool, so he appreciated better than most the unnerving effect of the electrifying atmosphere of Wembley, charged as it was on this occasion with high feeling for the club who by supreme endeavour had lifted themselves from the despair born of tragedy to play their part in the great show game of the season.

Lofthouse steadied the nerves of his colleagues in the most practical manner possible, with a goal in only the third minute. Although he played with a silver pin in an injured shoulder, he was the inspiration of his side and ten minutes after the interval he was credited with a second goal, one which caused some controversy at the time because he bundled goalkeeper Harry Gregg over the line with the ball.

Bolton had their escapes but this time the luck was on their side and it was a proud moment for Nat when he received the Cup from Prince Philip and was then chaired round the arena by his exuberant teammates.

Strangely it was as a substitute for a Manchester United player that Lofthouse had two years previously broken Steve Bloomer's 49-year-old record of 28 goals for England. It happened in Helsinki where England beat Finland 5–1. Two minutes from the interval, Tommy Taylor, the United leader who for three years had been one of Nat's great rivals for the centre-forward spot, was injured, and there were frantic signs to the referee that England wanted to make a change, as a substitution could only be made in the first half. For what seemed an agonising time the referee ignored the signals from the touchline and only seconds of the half remained when he waved Lofthouse on.

Lofthouse needed two goals to overtake Bloomer and his first did not come until 14 minutes from the end. Even then, many observers thought him offside when he shot the ball home. But the effort seven minutes later which gave him the record was undoubtedly the strangest of the 30 goals he scored in his 33 appearances for England.

From a left wing corner, Lofthouse headed towards the net but for once he had not connected squarely and it looked a tame effort. Dennis Wilshaw rushed forward to apply the finishing touch only to be blatantly held back by a Finnish defender. So the ball rolled loose and either the goalkeeper or a back could have cleared with ease but amazingly they left it to each other so that it rolled gently against a post and over the line, scarcely with enough force to reach the net.

Fluke or not, no one begrudged Lofthouse his triumph for here was one of soccer's gentlemen, never peevish when pulled up by the referee and never reacting to a bad foul against him with anything more than a look of pained surprise.

And after all, he could have had another scoring feat record to his name earlier if his colleagues had realised the position at the time. Lofthouse was in the Football League team that crushed the Irish League 7–1 at Wolverhampton in September 1952, with Nat helping himself to the first six goals. His shooting then was deadly, his sixth goal being a remarkable flick while running at full speed. Then, when the Football League was awarded a penalty it was Ramsey who took it because he had been delegated for any spot awards before the match. Lofthouse therefore had to be content with setting up an inter-league scoring record and being presented with the ball instead of an all-time international record. His name now stands beside that of Irishman Joe Bambrick, who netted six times in a full international against Wales in 1930 and the amateurs, W. C. Jordan and Vivian Woodward, who both achieved the six-goals-in-a-match feat for England before the first war.

It is not surprising that foreign clubs would have liked to entice Lofthouse away from Lancashire and before the 1953 Cup Final the Italian club, Florentina, offered him a three-year contract at £2,000 a year. But Bolton were so proud of their Nat, and rightly so, that in May 1957 they even waived a club rule dating back 34 years to keep him.

Lofthouse was given the chance of becoming host of the new Castle Hotel at Bolton and informed the club of his intention of taking the position since his soccer earnings had only been £15 plus win and draw bonuses and he had to consider his future. Under the club rules, no Bolton player could become a licensee and for a time it looked as though Nat and the club he had served with such distinction would part company. Though he was now past his peak transfer fees of £12,000 were quoted before Bolton decided that Lofthouse was worth more to them than the rule. As soon as it was rescinded in his case, Lofthouse happily re-signed.

The club need not have worried unduly for though the hotel was a swinging concern with Nat as a popular host he decided to give it up after less than two years. He and his wife Alma – the girl he had met when they were both eleven and he had dropped a snowball down her back – did not consider that the environment suited their children.

After breaking Bloomer's record Lofthouse was relegated to the international wilderness and was not even the reserve centre-forward for the World Cup in Sweden in 1958. But with England robbed of Tommy Taylor's services by the Munich crash, Lofthouse was recalled against the Russians at Wembley in October. Nat was in a panic before the game because he broke his left boot and borrowed a pair from Billy Wright. He played a blinder in a 5–0 victory and Wright never saw that pair back!

That season Lofthouse scored 29 more League goals for Bolton – a figure he had surpassed only once – to bring his total to 252 in 446 appearances but when the next campaign opened Bolton had to kick off without him. Nat had undergone an ankle operation during the summer and despite his strenuous efforts to regain fitness he reluctantly bowed to medical advice and retired in January 1960.

But Bolton and Lofthouse kept up their partnership and in December 1968 he was made manager, only the club's fourth in 50 years. And so his lifelong ambition has been achieved, for as a boy Lofthouse had vowed that he would always be in soccer somewhere. And soccer has been so glad to have Nat.

5
Bobby-Dazzler: Charlton

In these days of fluid soccer few players have a set function or a rigid area of activity on the field. They are taught to be jacks of all trades with even the goalkeeper an attacker in the sense that he is expected to use the ball rather than just aimlessly punt it out towards the centre spot. But no formation or system, however refined, will click if the men trying to adhere to it lack the necessary skill and industry. Of Jacks there are plenty; masters are a rarer breed.

That is why I sought out Bobby Charlton for inclusion in this parade of great leaders although he told me that he did not regard himself as a centre-forward in the accepted sense. The fact that he wore the number nine shirt and kicked off was purely coincidental. The truth is that Charlton is a centre-forward plus, a player of deft touches and explosive power, an artist of such perception that he spots angles instinctively and can distribute the ball with unerring accuracy. Add to those gifts an ability to deliver a shot of rocket-like intensity, often when far out and least expected. Many, many times Charlton has turned the tide of a match for England or Manchester United with just one of his 'specials'. For his shooting power alone, Bobby must rank as a great spearhead which is a prerequisite of a centre-forward and his scoring flair cannot be discounted merely because his versatility makes him not only a leader but a winger, inside forward and half-back as well.

Charlton was the son of an Ashington, Northumberland, miner whose wife came from one of the most remarkable soccer families, the Milburns, among whom his uncle, Jackie, played for Newcastle and England, and was regarded as one of the fastest centre-forwards the game has produced. But most of Bobby's early training came from his grandad, 'Tanner' Milburn, who prepared runners for the professional Powderhall sprint.

Not surprisingly, Bobby had no other thought than to be a professional footballer and there was a moment of consternation when he found himself booked for a grammar school which only played rugby. Fortunately his headmaster, who must be congratulated on his perception in realising that he had an embryo star on his hands, managed to switch him to Bedlington where they conformed to the association code and he developed so well that in 1953 he made his first appearance at Wembley, scoring twice for England Schoolboys against the Welsh.

This fixture is always a popular hunting ground for scouts and though Charlton was only 15 there was a queue of clubs eager to sign him. Newcastle, as his home club, were the obvious favourites, but Manchester United had already built up a reputation for their youth policy and it was there that Charlton went to become one of the Busby Babes.

Charlton was doing his National Service in the Army alongside his great pal, Duncan Edwards, when he was called up for his League debut against Charlton Athletic in October 1956. The club had been hit by injuries and Charlton himself was not fit. His right ankle was so swollen that when he went on the field he could not trust himself with a shot without jarring it, a discovery that had a crucial effect on his career for Bobby scored twice that day with his left and so convinced himself that when it came to finishing one foot was as good as the other.

At that time Tommy Taylor was at centre-forward with Charlton on his left and Taylor would undoubtedly have warranted a bigger reference here had he not been so tragically cut down when his career was in full flower. Since 1953, Taylor had rivalled Lofthouse among others for England caps and the 15 he won included two appearances in the World Cup in Switzerland in 1954.

In his first League season, Charlton played 14 games and scored ten times so that already he was building up a reputation as an eager marksman. United were front-runners in the First Division virtually throughout and carried off the championship for the second successive year. They reached the semi-final of the European Cup and when they fought through to the final of the F.A. Cup the double that had not been achieved for 60 years was within their grasp.

By a coincidence their opponents at Wembley were Aston Villa, who had been the last club to perform the double in the less demanding days of 1897, but from the sixth minute United were grievously handicapped by the loss of their goalkeeper, Ray Wood, who suffered a fractured cheekbone in a collision with Villa's Peter McParland. Charlton had clinched his place in the side by scoring in the semi-final against Birmingham but the only United player to feature on the Wembley score chart was Tommy Taylor who headed a great goal in a rousing rally after McParland had scored twice for Villa.

Rivalry was intense for places in the Manchester United side at that period and Charlton did not clinch a regular spot until Christmas 1957. The United attack had not been clicking as it should have done but its potency was proved in a most dramatic manner at Highbury the following February when they won a memorable League game 5–4. Two days later they set off for that ill-fated trip to Belgrade to meet Red Star in the second leg of a European Cup-tie.

On the return journey they put down at Munich for refuelling It was a raw, icy afternoon and twice the airliner taxied along the snow and slush without becoming airborne. The third attempt was fatal. Again the plane's wheels failed to leave the ground and this time there was no stopping as the plane hurtled on to crash with sickening force into the fence at the end of the runway.

As the airliner broke up so its occupants were hurled out and Charlton was one, still strapped to his seat. While eight of his teammates and three officials were fatally injured he escaped with little more than a scratch. That was the extent of the physical damage but the mental scar was inevitably much more serious. For the survivors there was only one remedy and that was to return to the job they knew and loved best as soon as they could. Charlton had gone to Europe as one of the babes of the side. From now on, he was to be one of the veterans, though the youngest of the survivors.

Charlton's work in the ensuing weeks not only helped makeshift United reach Wembley for the second year in succession but also earned him his first international cap against the Scots at Hampden Park, thus beginning a tremendous sequence which over the next 13 years saw him win more England honours than any other player in the game's history. Bobby has, in fact, played in every forward position for England except outside-right but on this occasion he was chosen at inside-right to Derek Kevan.

The Hampden game was memorable not merely because England's 4–0 victory was the widest margin they had gained on Scottish soil since 1888 but because Charlton scored a goal described by many as the best ever seen in that vast arena. Tom Finney made the opening for it, working down the left wing and then crossing straight into Charlton's path. Charlton rushing into the penalty area like an express at full throttle met the ball on the volley with his right foot and it zoomed chest-high into the net, which billowed out as if struck by a tornado. With volleys many will argue that there is always an element of fortune. Unless the timing is perfect the ball can go almost anywhere but this type of shot has become Charlton's stock in trade, a gift that has made him a deadly marksman, a man capable of shooting hard and straight without a moment's hesitation.

Throughout his career Charlton's explosive shooting has captured the imagination of the crowds. His lethal strikes have on occasion lifted both England and Manchester United to unexpected heights when, on the run of the play, they looked booked for defeat. Yet no player has adapted himself more readily to soccer's changing pattern. If he fell back when he first came into the game he was soon told to go back up front where he belonged. Then he became a midfield general, concentrating more on scheming openings for others, but though his own scoring opportunities dwindled the threat of that power-packed punch, delivered with searing accuracy from either foot, was always there. And Charlton has welcomed the changes. Each new role has brought a fresh challenge, a nettle he has grasped gladly to prevent himself lapsing into the stereotyped.

Charlton had his first look at world football when he was included in the World Cup squad in Sweden where he fretted on the sidelines while England battled through four matches in ten days before losing a group play-off against Russia. A hat-trick for Young England against Poland the following September prompted the selectors to recall him against Ireland and retain him against Russia whom England walloped 5–0 at Wembley for their first success in seven matches. In Billy Wright's 100th international against Scotland at Wembley it was Charlton's header that proved decisive and sealed a great occasion. The point is that Charlton had been picked as centre-forward for this game instead of inside-right as before and that is where he stayed against Italy and on the tour of South America which followed.

The last match of that tour, against the Americans in Los Angeles, was an unforgettable one for Bobby because the pitch was laid out in a baseball arena and the pitcher's mound was frequently the centre of operations for him. England thought the Americans would be a team of no-hopers but they had to revise their ideas when the home side scored first. That really roused the tourists who eventually won 8–1 with Charlton contributing three.

Midway between the 1959-60 season Charlton lost his form and was dropped both by his club and by England and that was something which, as far as United were concerned, was not to happen again for a decade. When he was recalled against Scotland it was as a left winger where he found far more space in which to manoeuvre than he had in the centre. Even so, it was not a position he relished for there were long periods when he saw little of the ball and others when he was called upon to make a long and unavailing dash for possession.

Still, it was as a left winger that Charlton stayed both for England while they averaged five goals a match in 1960–61 and in the World Cup in Chile, and when Manchester United beat Leicester City 3–1 to take the F.A. Cup back to Old Trafford for the second time since the war.

United chief Matt Busby developed Charlton as a midfield plotter and it was the number nine shirt that Bobby wore when he went on the continental tour that brought four victories in ten days and preceded England's World Cup triumph in 1966.

After a goalless draw against Uruguay, it needed a Charlton special to rekindle England's hopes and it came in the 38th minute of the game against Mexico. Until then a succession of England raids had bounced off the wall that the Mexicans set up in their penalty area. Then Charlton, receiving a pass from

Roger Hunt, scored a goal that was like the shock of a thunder-clap on a winter's evening. He took the ball forward a few paces and, with the Mexicans waiting for him to dribble on, he swung his right foot at the ball from 25 yards. It whistled into the net with such force that the goalkeeper was left stranded.

So Mexico were disposed of, and then France, to set the stage for the quarter-final against Argentina whose methods were such that when Charlton, or almost any other England player, beat an opponent he could expect to be tripped, body-checked, spat at or knocked to the ground. Geoff Hurst gave England victory with an expertly headed goal close on time, thus giving his side their ninth win from ten internationals. This result gripped the whole country with World Cup fever and the semi-final against Portugal went far to restore the prestige tarnished by the previous encounter. Charlton, nominally at inside-left this time, scored both goals in a 2–1 triumph that took England into their first World Cup final at their fifth attempt. Charlton's two goals were the most scored against that country and brought from them a dozen bottles of port, which are now among his most prized souvenirs in a collection built up during his world travels.

Charlton, playing behind three strikers – Geoff Hurst, Roger Hunt and Martin Peters – did not score on that proudest occasion in English football when in the electric atmosphere that was Wembley the World Cup was won on July 30th 1966. But of the part he played there can be no doubt. It was a match that England virtually won twice, for Germany equalised only seconds from the end of full time to earn not only a reprieve but what appeared a psychological advantage. That bitter blow when the Cup seemed in England's grasp, could have sapped all their spirit for that long gruelling final 30 minutes but instead an ecstatic crowd saw a resurgent England with Hurst scoring twice to become the first player to complete a hat-trick in a World Cup Final.

Yet, as if to be in that great side were not honour enough, further peaks were looming ahead for Charlton who that year was elected British and European footballer of the year.

In that year of 1966 long-cherished dreams for English football became reality. Charlton had earned every superlative that the soccer scribes could conjure. There was much more to him than sheer skill and artistry, though that often was enough to marvel at. No, Charlton brought to international football, both at representative and club level, a chivalry that many feared had been lost in the headlong pursuit of wealth and prestige. When the pace and the heat were at their greatest, Charlton never lost his serenity. Poised and always in control of himself, his behaviour was exemplary. Yet he was modest to a point where if the fans idolised him, as they have done frequently, he would look self-conscious and embarrassed, taken aback by it all and wanting for nothing more than to hasten to the peace and solitude of his Staffordshire home where he could relax with his wife and daughters. Charlton has been so utterly dedicated to the game, to England and to his club, it cannot be said that he did not work for fame. But that was just a by-product. And if you asked him the reason for his success he would always say it was the spirit of Manchester United, in which he is immensely proud, the guidance of people like Sir Matt Busby and Sir Alf Ramsey and the unselfish support of his team-mates.

But back to those superlatives because they all had to be dusted and brought out again in 1968 when Charlton's loyalty to United was rewarded with the captaincy and an eight-year contract which for a player of any age must be unique, let alone for one of 31.

In January he celebrated his 400th League game with a goal against West Ham, although it was his England colleague, Martin Peters, who was shadowing him. The following month against Spurs he missed a penalty. That sparked a succession of shots from him but Spurs managed to hold out until two minutes from the end when the score was 1–1.

Charlton was only just inside Spurs' territory when he gathered a pass from Francis Burns. In a sprint of 40 yards, his speed and control took him past four defenders. As he veered to the right Pat Jennings came out to narrow the angle, yet Charlton still managed to squeeze the ball between the goalkeeper and post, hitting it fiercely into the far corner from 12 yards.

The match against Sweden at Wembley was memorable in

that Charlton scored his 45th goal for England, thus overtaking the previous record of Jimmy Greaves. His effort helped England to a 3–1 win and it was fitting that his name should figure on the scoresheet for he was the only survivor from either side of those that had played there nine years earlier. Again it was a superb individual effort which dwarfed every other incident in the game. He beat two opponents, feinted to shoot with his left, dragged the ball to his right to evade another challenge and then crashed it home from more than 20 yards.

Of all the triumphs in which he shared, it is doubtful if any have given him greater satisfaction and delight than that on 29th May when he proudly led out Manchester United, the first English club ever to reach the final of the European Cup, to do battle with Benfica. And battle was the word for it.

After netting 18 times in his first 26 European Cup-ties Charlton had not scored in ten games against continental opposition, not scored in fact since a previous game against Benfica in Lisbon two years earlier. So the omens did not appear bright.

The first half was literally foul. Charlton was a victim but never a perpetrator of the sheer physical clashes which brought a succession of free kicks as tempers were whipped to boiling point. It was sad to see such a great occasion sullied and the teams disappeared down the tunnel at the interval to a storm of booing.

Only a few minutes had gone in the second half when Charlton rubbed out the memory of what had gone before with a glorious back header from David Sadler's cross. United were in front and there they stayed. It seemed the trophy was theirs and then, with barely ten minutes left, Benfica equalised, forcing extra time.

But it was United who best summoned up all their reserves of skill and energy as in the last pulsating 30 minutes they crashed three more goals into the Benfica net, with Charlton scoring the last.

Wembley went crazy with joy. As Charlton forgot his aching body to collect the huge trophy he could reflect that every major honour the game had to offer was now his. Almost overcome with emotion it is not surprising that when the lap round the stadium came, so that delirious supporters could pay homage to their heroes, Charlton handed over the Cup to two of his colleagues and trotted round wearily in the rear.

The services Charlton has rendered to the nation's soccer were royally acclaimed in January 1969 when he was awarded an OBE. And still the honours came. When he was capped for the 100th time at Wembley in April, 1970, the giant scoreboard lit up with the greeting 'Congratulations to Bobby'. He signalled the occasion with yet another goal in England's 3–1 win over Northern Ireland, and a china firm based in his home county produced a special set of 750 plates bearing his portrait and the names of the countries he has played against.

It was against West Germany in the quarter-finals of the World Cup in June that Charlton overhauled Billy Wright's record of 105 caps. England were two goals ahead when Bobby was withdrawn from the heat of that game in Leon and without him his side went down to a 3–2 defeat, thus giving the Germans revenge for their setback in the final four years earlier.

Even after the heat of Mexico and the altitude problems it presented there was only a brief respite from soccer for Charlton. He went to Australia for a coaching clinic in Sydney and then at last came a real break, a leisurely return through the Pacific and out of range of telephone or television.

Early in the new season, Charlton, to the consternation but surely not to the surprise of United, seemed to be losing some of his flair. He was dropped from the first team while he regained his master touch. Quickly the batteries were recharged and on the eve of his 33rd birthday he made his 500th appearance for his club against Crystal Palace at Old Trafford. But Palace not only beat United but kept Bobby waiting for the goal he needed to beat Jack Rowley's club record of 198.

Charlton has played against 30 different countries and against each of the home countries at least ten times and he has scored three goals in an international four times – against the U.S. in Los Angeles in May, 1959; Luxembourg, October 1960; Mexico at Wembley in May, 1961; and Switzerland in Basle in June, 1963.

If Charlton is asked what is left his likely reply is: 'What else is there? What better way is there of making a living?'

Charlton's hope is that the game will always have a niche for him. Few can doubt that soccer will be the poorer if it fails to provide one.

6

Drake - The galloping Gunner Smith - The bulldozing Spur

Cricket followers were first to appreciate the power and possibilities of Ted Drake. The crowd basking in the sunshine at Southampton that late August day in 1931 had just clapped the newcomer into the pavilion. The strapping youngster with the dark hair parted almost down the middle had just shared a stand of 86 with Phil Mead against Glamorgan. Nor had he been overshadowed by Hampshire's great left-handed batting maestro for his share was 45 and the runs had flowed at more than one a minute.

Drake worked as a mechanical apprentice at Southampton gasworks but his love was sport – soccer in winter, first for Southampton Boys and then Winchester City, cricket in summer. He became a man of superb physique, with big shoulders, a strong body, great thighs and sturdy legs. And in temperament he was utterly fearless.

Southampton spotted him easily enough. They couldn't very well miss this lad who was the talk of local defences as he cleaved through them like a destroyer's bow parting the waves. By 1932 he was in their League side, marking his debut with a hat-trick, by the end of the next campaign he had topped their scoring list with 21 goals and by the time he signed for Arsenal in April 1934 he had added another 22 in 27 games.

Yet though a fee of £5,000 changed hands, a record at that time for a Southampton player, it took all the persuasive powers of the late George Allison to persuade Drake to leave the Dell for Highbury. He was at that time a shy, diffident young man to whom the bright lights of London held no appeal though he was being given the chance to join the club that was the talk of soccer. For these were halcyon days for Arsenal. Beginning with their Cup Final success over Huddersfield in 1930, they had won the League twice in three seasons, were poised to win it

HUGHIE GALLACHER . . . 'There was not much of him. He stood only 5 foot 5 inches and his boots were size 6½. But they were two sticks of dynamite'

JACKIE MILBURN . . . 'In the gallery of great players who never let up, Jackie deserves a prominent place'

NAT LOFTHOUSE . . .
'Took only one route to goal – the shortest'

BOBBY CHARLTON . . . 'Another volley from that lethal left foot'

again, and had reached Wembley again only to go down by a disputed goal to Newcastle.

Only a few months previously, Arsenal had paid out £8,000 for another centre-forward, Jimmy Dunne, but it was Drake who captured the imagination of critical terrace fans. They were conditioned to almost non-stop success and regarded Allison's hunch as an unnecessary gamble. As for Drake himself, he attributed his meteoric rise at Highbury to the club's spirit and training routines which included work in a shooting box where the marksmen could sharpen their aim.

Drake was a player of boundless energy. Although no mean craftsman, he never bothered about finesse, always taking the shortest route to goal, and he was lucky to have on each side of him two arch schemers in Alex James and Ray Bowden who were supreme at opening the way. Here was no lightweight infantry sniper; Drake was like a piece of mobile artillery, remorseless in his approach, never giving up the chase until the quest was far beyond the bounds of normal hopelessness, and never losing his confidence or dash despite the injuries which were the natural corollary of the risks he took.

Within little more than a month of Drake's arrival Arsenal had won the League title and they went on to complete the First Division's only hat-trick apart from that of Huddersfield between 1923 and 1926.

By November 1934 Drake was an England player. He was the type of centre-forward everyone could understand, so uncompromising was his method. Drake the dauntless he was dubbed and no name was more richly earned. There were times when he was carried off unconscious only to return minutes later, times when he was cut and bruised, a time when he broke two wrist bones and carried on with them strapped and an occasion when he was borne off by Tom Whittaker, who succeeded Allison as manager, with his head swathed in a towel after a collision.

That first England game was a memorable one for Drake as he was one of seven Arsenal players included in the side against Italy and it was a real home match for them as it was staged at Highbury. In 20 minutes England were three goals up. It was then that the Italians evidently decided that more robust tactics were called for and in the later stages of the game it was a case of England being represented by the walking wounded as they were pulled back to 3–2. The match provided an early example of how, when there is too much at stake, sportsmanship is likely to become a bad second to the need to win at whatever cost, for the Italians had been spurred on by some glittering inducements from Mussolini.

Drake became a special target for their attentions, especially after he had committed what was in their eyes the unpardonable crime of charging the goalkeeper. Ted was fed up with seeing the Italian goalkeeper bouncing the ball to the edge of the penalty area unmolested so he challenged him. Immediately a posse of Italian defenders surrounded him and one grabbed him round the neck.

The day that earned Drake a permanent niche in the record books came at Villa Park in December 1935. Here was the team of the midlands playing the team of London that had carried off the League championship four times in the past five years. What a soccer feast it promised to be and a crowd of 60,000 packed the terraces as the sides came out.

When Drake ran on to the field Arsenal fans noted with some consternation that his left knee was heavily bandaged. In ordinary circumstances he would not have been playing for he had twisted it badly in the previous game. But the circumstances were not ordinary. Two days earlier he had visited the Royal Northern Hospital where the sick Allison had told Drake that the best tonic he could give him would be two points from the Villa match.

Soon Drake was labouring under a further handicap. He chased a ball out to the wing where it went over the line and on to the red track. He followed to gather it but he was wearing rather long studs because the going was greasy on top and these bit on the hard ground pitching him forward so that he landed flat on his face. He grazed both arms and felt a 'ripe twerp' as the crowd around guffawed.

So one of the greatest stories in the history of soccer had a farcical preface, for from that moment Drake's shooting was even more venomous than usual. His first six shots were all goals, the seventh hit the underside of the bar, bounced down and struck someone before being scrambled clear, and the eighth was another goal. Not since J. Ross had performed the feat for Preston 47 years earlier had a player notched seven goals in a

First Division match and it has not been done since. Yet the 7–1 result belied the exchanges for the match was not that one-sided and Drake admitted that the eight shots he had were all that he was allowed.

Drake's scoring blitz began in the 15th minute when he took Pat Beasley's pass, eluded Tommy Griffiths and banged the ball home. After 28 minutes, Drake had to brush aside two challenges, those from Griffiths and Cummings, before he was clear to net with a brilliant shot. Six minutes later a drive by Beasley cannoned off a defender and Villa must have wondered what they had done to upset the fates when the ball landed at Drake's feet. Almost inevitably, he cracked it home without hesitation.

As far as Villa were concerned the second half was even more disastrous for Drake completed his second hat-trick of the game in 12 minutes. The first was an extraordinary effort for it looked as though a centre was going harmlessly over the by-line. At least, that's what Griffiths thought and he left it, but Drake tore up like an express at full throttle, pulled the ball back and flicked it past the goalkeeper from an 'impossible' angle.

The second came when Drake finished off a thrust by Bowden and Bastin with a shot that left the despairing Villa goalkeeper stranded, and the third when he pounced on a partial clearance. For half an hour there was then a respite for Villa which really highlighted this incredible match, for the midlanders had as much of the play as Arsenal. They had spent a fortune on international players in a fight to avoid relegation and had dropped one of Drake's closest friends, Jimmy Allen, a £10,000 centre-half, so that Griffiths, a Welsh international signed from Middlesbrough for another big fee, could mark him. In addition, Arsenal played more to a defensive formation, relying on quick breakaways.

As one critic summed up afterwards the only difference between the sides was Drake who, in the last minute, was put clear again by Bastin and went roaring through for his fourth goal of the half and seventh in all.

To Drake, the most memorable thing about the match was the sportsmanship of the Villa players and officials. They insisted on him having the ball, signed by the team, and of all his souvenirs there was none he treasured more. But Drake's great match was not achieved without him paying a heavy price. At the end, he limped off in pain from his damaged knee and later in the season, after a further breakdown while playing for England against Wales, had to undergo an operation.

There was a real danger that he would miss the 1936 Cup Final against Sheffield United but Drake willed himself back to fitness in the six weeks that were available to him. First he played in a friendly against Cambridge University and then in a Combination game before it was decided to risk him in a League match. By an ironic chance it was the return game with Villa at Highbury a week before the Final. This time there was no goal-glut for Drake but the one he did net was enough to plunge Villa into the Second Division for the first time in their long history. If any goal gave Drake mixed feelings that was the one, the time when he needed a goal and yet wished that it had not been at Villa's expense.

A week later Drake set the seal on his great season by driving home a centre from Bastin for the only goal to win a Cup medal and bring the trophy back to Highbury. The pity is that Drake has no medal to gaze on today. It was among a collection of precious souvenirs that he lent to the organisers of a fête. They locked them in a safe but this was forced open and Drake's collection has not been traced since.

Drake had a largely frustrating afternoon that day at Wembley for the Sheffield defence was magnificent. When the chance came, and it was just about his only one, he had the briefest glance of the ball. 'Instinct must have guided my foot,' he said later. 'Because next moment there was that Wembley roar and it sounded wonderful to me.'

Such a forceful leader was Drake that he even persuaded the Hungarians to change their style. The Magyars had been reluctant to adopt the third back game, preferring to base their tactics more on the old-style attacking centre-half, but having been walloped 6–2 at Highbury with Drake in the van they realised that against men of his calibre their policy was tantamount to committing soccer suicide.

In 1938, Drake married Ruby Maggs, the girl he had met at a dance while still working at Southampton gasworks, and on the tenth anniversary of his seven-goal feat she presented him with their third son, Graham.

During the war Drake served in the RAF but continued to play for the Gunners until, in 1945, he suffered the spinal injury which was to end his career. It was not until after he had played several more matches with the back strapped that the slipped disc trouble was diagnosed. His movements were so restricted that a colleague had to tie the laces of his football boots as Ted could not bend to reach them.

In 168 First Division appearances for Arsenal between 1934 and 1939 he scored 123 goals and his hat-trick against Hungary helped him to a total of six goals in his five internationals. No doubt there would have been more if men of the calibre of George Camsell and latterly Tommy Lawton had not been among his contempories.

If the playing door shut on Drake at Elm Park it was there that another one opened when he became manager of Reading in 1947. And he proved such a success that five years later he was appointed to succeed Billy Birrell as manager of Chelsea. Drake set about solving the mystery of the Chelsea enigma. Here was a club that over the years had fielded some of the greatest stars in the game. But many were individuals and Chelsea had rarely blended into a team.

Drake scorned the big cheque, paying modest fees for little-known players at the threshold of their careers while staking his reputation on a youth policy. Drake's Ducklings gained almost as wide publicity as the Busby Babes and gradually he rammed all the old Pensioners' jokes down the comedians' throats. Chelsea had not been higher than 13th in the six seasons since the war but high noon came for them in their golden jubilee year of 1955 when they won the championship, four points clear of their nearest challengers, Wolves and Portsmouth.

Perhaps they were forced up, rather like a hothouse plant, for Chelsea found it tough at the top and though Drake brought the same infectious enthusiasm to management that he had to playing he could not again repeat that success.

It was a disenchanted Drake therefore, that walked away from Stamford Bridge that bleak December day in 1961 when he parted company not only with Chelsea but with the game he had ornamented for 32 years, and instead turned his attention to running a betting shop. His departure cleared the way for Tommy Docherty to begin his turbulent reign and eight years passed before Ted was lured back to soccer. Then he became manager and coach to Vic Buckingham, the former Spur, in Barcelona where he spent much of his time, as he had begun, seeking young talent.

Perhaps it would have been different at Chelsea if Drake had been able to keep his young starlets – men like Bobby Smith, for example, for Smith was no keener to move from Chelsea than Drake himself had been to leave Southampton, and, like Nat Lofthouse, he became a centre-forward by accident rather than design.

Smith was as near Drake in method and style as any centre-forward is ever likely to be. He was the bulldozer of Tottenham, the brawn among the brains of that great side who achieved the Cup and League double in 1960–61. Smith fittingly gained all the honours for he had caps against Scotland, Wales and Ireland to put beside his Cup and championship medals.

The black tousle-headed Smith had the physique one might expect of a lad brought up in a forge and spending a year working down a pit. He was born at the village of Lingdale, near Redcar, and it was on the racecourse that he played his early soccer for the local boys' club, not at centre-forward but at right-back.

One day illness prevented the regular leader from playing. The side had a reserve back but no deputy up front so Bobby volunteered for the job. Not long afterwards a Chelsea scout saw him bang in four goals out of six in the first half and promptly invited him to London for a trial. But Bobby was quickly disenchanted with the metropolis. Just two games in the junior side and he hared back to the open spaces of the North Riding only to be promptly ordered to return by an irate father.

Smith made his League debut in the same season that he signed as a professional and was soon hailed as soccer's new wonder boy. Jack Fairbrother, the Newcastle goalkeeper, described him as the most accurate marksman he had played against. Such praise so early was premature but as a prediction it proved much closer the mark.

It is never easy for a youngster to come into a struggling side and that was Bobby's lot, being called upon when Chelsea had taken only four points from nine matches. What is more, Drake had a surfeit of centre-forwards, or rather men who could occupy that position, despite the fact that Smith worked up excellent credentials by heading the club's Combination scores for two years.

Some of his critics at that time did not believe that National Service helped his cause. He spent his second year of it stationed at Victoria, which was convenient enough, but the Army life was blamed for him losing his speed and timing. So Smith was only a first team casual rather than a regular when, in December 1955, he was called from the games room where he had been playing snooker, to Drake's office below it and told he could go to Spurs.

The fee mentioned of £20,000 was a big one. Even so, it was remarkable that the deal went through for Drake was not eager to part and Smith was not keen to go. Drake's trouble was in finding justification for playing Smith when he had such experienced leaders as Roy Bentley, Ron Tindall, Jim Lewis and Les Stubbs to call on. He had already rejected offers from nearly a dozen clubs.

As for Smith, he liked Chelsea. Furthermore, he had married at the age of 21 and he and his wife, Mavis, were busy setting up a home in West London. But what persuaded him that the bus ride to Tottenham was worthwhile was the promise that he would step straight into the League side.

Tottenham immediately began grafting skill in using the ball and a keen positional sense on to Smith's bustle and resolution. Special exercises made him quicker off the mark and sharper on the turn. He was encouraged to go and meet the ball instead of running away from it and whenever he wandered out to the wings it was never without a purpose.

By 1958 he was Spurs' leading goal scorer and being freely tipped as an England centre-forward. Indeed, he was picked for the World Cup squad that went to Sweden in 1958 when he had the bitter disappointment of seeing his team go down without being given the opportunity to kick a ball in their defence.

It was not until October 1960 that England at last recognised the ability of this rugged, husky goal menace by picking him for the game against Ireland in Belfast and he repaid them with six goals in four games. The most memorable of these occasions was the game against Spain on a soggy Wembley pitch. In such stamina-sapping conditions, Smith was England's powerhouse. They leaned heavily on him and he did not fail them although he had every excuse so vicious were some of the challenges against him. Twice England went ahead and twice Spain equalised. Then midway through the second half, Smith headed his side back into the lead and clinched the match with one of Wembley's great goals eight minutes from the end.

Smith had just been kicked in the stomach. He was still feeling the effects when the ball came and he shaped to burst past the centre-half. As he sidestepped two challenges he heard Johnny Haynes calling for the ball. Looking up, Smith noted that there was a Spaniard between them who could intercept and the goalkeeper was racing out. So he calmly chipped the ball over the head of the advancing rival with such precision that it dropped neatly under the bar and into the far corner of the net.

Already that season he had kicked off with 13 goals in his first eight games and when he scored the first of a hat-trick against Blackpool in September he achieved a club scoring record, beating the 138 set up by another fine Tottenham and England centre-forward, George Hunt. His total then of 141 had taken only 191 matches to compile, a much faster rate than Hunt had accomplished.

Four more goals came to Smith in Spurs' amazing 13–2 victory over Crewe in an F.A. Cup replay but then his touch seemed to desert him and he failed to find the net in seven of his next ten games. Smith took such failings very hard for he thought he was the player to blame for Spurs' faltering in the championship race of the previous season when they finished third, two points behind Burnley and one behind Wolves.

He was dropped for the visit to Everton and when that game was lost was promptly recalled to face his old pals at Chelsea. That afternoon everything came off for him and he scored all three goals in a 3–1 win. Next, against Manchester City, he had as many chances, only to be foiled by the catlike agility of Bert Trautmann and when Chelsea took their revenge with a 1–0 success at Tottenham, Spurs dropped from the top of the table and never regained it.

Smith determined to buckle down to it, setting out with the

aim of scoring at least a goal a game. But he need not have worried for there were others scoring goals alongside him, such as Les Allen, Cliff Jones and Terry Dyson, powered on by Danny Blanchflower and Dave Mackay, probably the greatest pair of club wing-halves in the history of the game. Apart from winning the championship and the Cup, Spurs began the campaign with eleven successive wins, went on to a record 31, with 16 away, and equalled Arsenal's First Division record tally of 66 points. For all his lean periods, Smith finished top scorer with 32 and added the vital first goal in the 2–0 Cup Final success over Leicester.

Even our greatest players are not immune to the ebb and flow of fortune's tide and a knee injury forced him that May to miss the 8–0 trouncing of Mexico against whom, his deputy, Gerry Hitchens, of Aston Villa, scored in the first minutes of his international career. It seemed that no harm had been done as far as Smith was concerned when he was recalled for the next of these World Cup qualifying games against Portugal but when England managed only a 1–1 draw in Lisbon, Smith lost his place – the first voluntary team change for nearly a year.

The bulky Smith then decided that as he had not made any plans for a summer holiday he would spend the time slimming. He went on a self-imposed liquid diet which was so rigorous that he lost a stone and a half in six weeks. By the time he reported back for training at Tottenham he was down to a modest 12 stone 12lb but the new slimline Smith presented but a frail threat to opposing goalkeepers compared with the old. By the middle of December 1960 he had scored 24 goals; in the same period of the next season he managed just four, one against Blackpool on the opening day, one against Cardiff in September and two against Gornik in the European Cup. Then blank. A frightening period when he was passed over not only by the England selectors but by Spurs as well.

Smith decided that there was only one answer – to eat his way back to form. He threw his diet sheet away and began a Billy Bunter campaign with Mavis feeding him up with his old favourites like steak and kidney pudding, and stews with dumplings. Gradually the scoring touch returned and after 12 weeks in the reserves an injury to Les Allen gave Smith the chance to make his comeback against Nottingham Forest in February.

Goals to a centre-forward are like water to a traveller crossing the desert and Smith rushed eagerly for his oasis. He scored in that comeback match, added two more against West Bromwich in the Cup and another two against the Czech side, Dukla, in the European Cup.

It seemed that Smith was all set to scale a new peak when he and Jimmy Greaves, who had become known as Spurs' smash-and-grab specialists, were called up by England to face the Scots at Hampden in April of 1962. The match was crucial, as England were only three matches and two months away from the World Cup in Chile and Smith especially, having been reduced to a place on the sidelines in 1958, wanted to do well. Perhaps he was too anxious. Whatever the reason for his poor game, there was no fairytale ending as the Scots powered to their first Hampden victory over England since 1937.

When the party to be taken to Chile was announced Smith alone of that beaten side was excluded. He had played no worse than some of his colleagues but, as against Portugal in the World Cup preliminaries the previous season, he was made the scapegoat. Ironically, that match in Scotland was the first time Smith had finished on the losing side in an international.

Once again Smith began the long arduous climb up the slippery slope and after just nine first team games for Spurs he was recalled by England to lead the line against France in the European Nations Cup clash in Paris in February 1963. England lost then, but there was no axe for Smith this time and he was still the man in possession when the following February Spurs manager, Billy Nicholson, surprised the London soccer world by buying wing-half Laurie Brown from Arsenal and putting him straight into the League side at centre-forward. And as Brown led his new club to a 3–1 win over his old, Smith just hid in the crowd and watched.

Brown's first nine games for Spurs brought just one goal and by the middle of April Smith was back. But he was given only one first team outing before hearing the bitter news that Spurs were in the market for offers.

Big-hearted Smith had nine seasons with Spurs, including the greatest years in the history of the club. For five of those campaigns he was their top scorer and though in the latter part his scoring slowed to a trickle he nevertheless mustered 176.

Thirteen more goals came in his 15 internationals, the last being against Northern Ireland at Wembley the previous November when he was among the scorers in an 8–3 victory. Ten days later he scored for Spurs in a home League game against Sheffield Wednesday and he had not found the net since in first class football.

Even so, clubs quickly joined the queue for his services, and the offers were not restricted to England. St. Mirren were prepared to pay the bargain price of £5,000 and so, too, were the Dutch club, Ajax. Finally Smith settled for Fourth Division Brighton and so, instead of going on a 12,540-mile soccer tour to Lisbon, New York and Rio with the England party, which he could have done if he had kept his place at Tottenham, he travelled that May day just the 100 miles to the South coast and back.

His arrival certainly braced up Brighton. Season ticket sales doubled, the club began with their biggest gate since their Second Division days six years earlier and Smith duly rewarded them with two headed goals in a 3–1 win over Barrow. With just this one personality purchase, Albion achieved the best home and away attendance record in the Fourth Division and their own average gate rose by 7,000. Such was the hefty handful, the hell-raising centre-forward that was Bobby Smith.

He found the going tougher. There were always two men marking him and he missed the atmosphere that a packed White Hart Lane created. Still he was satisfied that he was doing a good job and he soon moved from London to a bungalow at Shoreham.

Now it was time for Bobby to meet up with Crewe again and it was there in January 1965 that he received a serious thigh injury.

For six weeks he was on the sidelines and even when he was fully fit there was no rush to restore him to the first team. Yet Brighton soared on to achieve their aim of winning the Fourth Division championship and the grand start Smith gave them with 20 goals provided a solid foundation.

His success with Brighton prompted the top Austrian club, FC Vienna, to make a £7,000 offer for him but when he crossed the Channel to play in a trial for them against Celtic, their coach admitted that the club could not afford him. The trial was a fiasco and Smith was bitter that Brighton seemed prepared to sell him after the part he had played in their revival. The trouble was that Bobby now had to renew his battle with the scales, for his weight had risen to 15st 7lb and Brighton suggested he should fight the battle of the bulge at a health centre to trim off a stone and a half.

Smith had played only one match for Brighton in the 1965 season when he and the club parted company, apparently over the question of some newspaper articles. A month after leaving Brighton, he joined Hastings of the Southern League, signing a contract that guaranteed him £65 a week – the highest paid to a player outside the Football League.

Once again history was repeated with Smith giving his new club the boost they were seeking. A typically rousing start brought him five goals in his first three appearances and though he then failed to score in his next eight games he was laying them on so well for his colleagues that the club were soon in the promotion hunt.

Within three months, Hastings were being pestered to part with their new asset. This time it was a South African club that was taking a keen interest in him but the overtone was never seriously followed up and the tempestuous Smith entered on one of the less happy periods of his career.

Eventually Hastings became so exasperated with their temperamental star that they dismissed him in April after he had scored eleven goals in 19 games for them. Bobby successfully appealed to the Southern League against his dismissal. Unhappily, the reprieve was short-lived. The club reported that there were no offers for him, when he was put up for sale with the rest of the players in an economy drive, and when the club let him go a second time for an alleged breach of training regulations the League this time upheld their action.

Nothing came either of a reported offer of £85 a week from San Francisco for the man who, three years earlier, had been England's centre-forward. So he then tried to break into management as successor to his old Spurs' colleague, Terry Medwin, at Cheshunt but the club informed him that they were not yet ready to make a new appointment. So Bobby suffered one frustration after another. He had always been one for a gamble, saying once that he would put his last penny on a three-legged donkey in the Grand National in the hope that all the others would fall, and now the wheel of fortune was spinning violently against him.

When the 1967 season opened there was the now somewhat portly Bobby Smith plodding round the track at Stamford Bridge, back at the ground where he first made his name. It was a nostalgic sight seeing this great player back on square one. Tommy Docherty had given him permission to use the Chelsea facilities and Smith hoped that by losing a stone and scaling down to his old playing weight he might yet, at 33, break back into League football.

But the hope seems to have faded and since he left Hastings this great player's still considerable talents have been seen only in charity matches.

7
Charles and Ford: The Wizards of Wales

Put an ordinary soccer mortal in the red shirt of Wales and he becomes a fire-cracker . . . fizzing, buzzing and explosive. Frequently the dauntless men from the Principality have played in a manner far above their station. Yet there are some who have not required the inspiration of that red shirt to reach the peaks, some for whom the word great would be no exaggeration whatever colours they donned. Of such a calibre are Trevor Ford and John Charles, two giants from the valleys whose potential, ironically, was so tardily recognised that Welsh clubs did not enjoy their services at the most glittering stages of their careers.

Ford's career in the Welsh international side began with a Victory appearance against Ireland in 1946 and finished eleven years later – which meant that he did not play for his country the first time they reached the final stages of the World Cup in Sweden in 1958.

Charles, who like Ford, was born in Swansea but seven years his junior, joined Trevor in the international side in 1950 when, just over 18, he was the youngest player ever to appear for Wales. That began a career for his country which spanned 15 years but although he did play in the 1958 World Cup he was then attuned to the different pace and ploys of Italian football and could not adapt himself to the sudden transition that his colleagues demanded.

The difference in approach of these two men provided a fascinating study. Ford was all fire, tempestuous and rumbustious, a man of tremendous energy whose sheer physical aggression made many goalkeepers apprehensive.

Ford was completely fearless. He would go in hard, and he took many hard knocks in return. Sparing himself or his rivals just never occurred to him. Yet his approach was always open. There was nothing sly, nothing of the trickster or artful dodger in his make-up, and he was rarely in trouble with the referees.

The approach of Charles was different, the secret here being that he was a late developer in the physical sense. In his early teens he stood 5ft. 4in. and weighed no more than ten stone. There was no point in him barging into goalkeepers and centre-halves because the likelihood was that he would just bounce off with no more effort than a tennis ball hitting a brick wall. His father implored him always to play football and not be a basher so that right from the outset he was encouraged to put skill and judgment first.

The philosophy of gentle John was that it was far better to take the goals as they came than blunder into opponents and perhaps be the unwitting cause of an injury that could end a career. It is rare that a goalkeeper makes a point of racing up to the opposing centre-forward at the end of a game to shake his hand, not just as a feeble offhand token of sportsmanship but with warm sincerity. But it happened to Charles more than once.

Shortly before the end of a League game with Doncaster, Charles had a chance to end a goalless deadlock. He raced for a through ball although he realised that the goalkeeper, Ken Hardwick, would – or should – reach it first. Such was Charles' acceleration that there was little in it and Hardwick had to dive at his feet. As he gathered the ball to him, he braced himself for a numbing collision but in that fleeting moment, where there is no time for thought but only to act by instinct and upbringing, he sensed but never felt the presence of Charles.

With the poise and balance of a dancer, Charles took off and cleared the prostrate goalkeeper who was quick to appreciate the physical feat that it entailed.

Another difference between the two men was that Ford believed himself to be a centre-forward and nothing else. He disliked any change of position so much that he once declined to play inside-right to Gerry Hitchens at Cardiff, saying that he would sooner lead the reserves attack than play out of his proper place in the League side. Charles, on the other hand, said that he would play for his club or country wherever he was needed. He was, in fact, the complete all-round footballer.

As a centre-forward, Ford had an insatiable desire to bang the ball into the opponents' net and he was prepared to take any legal means to achieve that objective. Charging of the goalkeeper was permitted providing he was holding the ball and had both feet on the ground. Ford believed in charging, in nagging the goalkeeper by blocking and chasing at every opportunity. With his broad and powerful shoulders, it is not surprising that many goalkeepers did not relish his challenges and the fans on visiting grounds liked it even less. That is how Ford became the target of the boo boys yet, in front of his own supporters, he was a hero, for they recognised him for the great-hearted trier he always was. He was a dynamic champion of lost causes, prepared to do battle against packed defences single-handed if necessary, always robust but never guilty of a shabby foul. He believed that a centre-forward, as the most closely marked man on the field, had to develop a Houdini flair for wriggling out of tight corners, but Ford's assets were not so much his control, although that developed over the years, as his speed, strength and shooting power. Ford could not match the all-round versatility of Charles – very few could – but what he lacked in subtlety he made up by being a thunderbolt.

One common denominator between both players was that the Army helped to make them. Ford went in a gangling youngster of 5ft. 9in. and weighing just about nine stone. He came out two inches taller and three stones heavier. For a time during the war he was stationed at Shoeburyness and appeared as a guest player for Clapton Orient at wing-half. But it was the Army who hit the jackpot with him. They played him out of position – at centre-forward!

Whereas many athletes were critical of the Army way of life, Charles admits that it not only improved his standard of play but helped to build him up physically as well. He had been putting on weight in the wrong places and that was quickly trimmed off. In addition, he found that if he took part in basketball sessions it would release him from some of the less pleasant fatigues and Charles believes that much of his later exceptional ability in the air stemmed from the leaping about he had to do. When he was sent to Carlisle his team won the Army Football Cup it was there that he developed cartilage trouble requiring operations on both knees. The surgeons must

TED DRAKE . . . 'was like a piece of mobile artillery, remorseless in his approach'

BOBBY SMITH . . . 'all bustle and resolution'

JOHN CHARLES . . . 'the poise and balance of a dancer'

TREVOR FORD . . . 'all fire, tempestuous and rumbustious, a man of tremendous energy'

have done an excellent job for his mobility was never later impaired as a result.

The fascinating careers of these two great leaders is worth studying in closer detail so let us start with Ford, since, being the elder, he was the first to jump to prominence. As a Swansea boy, he was the youngest and smallest in the Townhill team but his rugged approach made up for his lack of inches and he was played at left-back. He made such a good job of it that he was chosen for the Welsh Boys' team, only to be deprived of his cap by a broken leg.

Wolves made him an offer but Ford felt that his future was bound up in Wales. He went to Vetch Field where he was tried at full-back and wing-half before settling down in the forward line.

Even Arsenal offered him amateur forms, but he never signed them, preferring to keep them as a souvenir instead, and Cardiff must have felt aggrieved for they recognised his potential although realising that they had little chance since Ford's father was connected with Swansea.

In the regional competition just after the war, Ford scored 41 goals – top of the four divisions – out of Swansea's 90 and it seemed that the club would want to hold their young protégé whatever the cost. But Ford was a restless individualist. With League football back in full swing he felt that only a club in the top flight would serve, and a haggle over how he should prepare for a cup-tie provided the background for Swansea's decision to part and his transfer to Aston Villa in exchange for a £10,000 fee.

So Ford moved to the midlands but his heart was still in Wales, so much so that when the time came for the arrival of his first son, David, he sent his wife, Louise, to Swansea so that the boy could be born a Welshman.

Ford did not find the transition easy. His form was so wretched that he decided to start afresh and spent hours practising alone to develop the skills necessary for soccer in the First Division. But his dedication paid off. There were 17 goals in 1947–48, 13 the next year when he played in four fewer League games and 18 in 1949–50, and what is more he had become a fixture in the international side.

But ten games at the start of the 1950–51 campaign brought

only two goals and Ford thought that a change of club would bring a change of luck. Welshmen were elated at the possibility of Ford moving back to one of their clubs so their chagrin can be imagined when the transfer took him even further away – to Sunderland. This time the fee was a record £30,000 but the magnet was a house by the sea and the offer of a job outside the game which gave him security.

And then there was the strange incident when Ford, as he has related himself, was invited to rummage around in a part of the deserted stand at night and find something to his advantage.

It was the third time in 45 years that Sunderland had been involved in a record transfer. In 1905, they received the first ever four-figure fee from Middlesbrough for Alf Common and in 1948, two years before the Ford deal, they became the first £20,000 spenders when they signed Len Shackleton from Newcastle. For 17 days clubs all over the country rivalled each other for Ford's signature but to Roker Park he went.

When I met Ford in London last year he told me: 'The career of a professional footballer is not a long one and he never knows when it is going to be cut short, especially in a case like mine, because a man with my style of play takes some knocks in his time. I know, I had plenty. A man owes it to himself and his family to go out for the best terms possible. You must remember the "slave" conditions of those times. By the time I signed for Sunderland £40,000 had been paid for my services but the highest wage I could earn was £15.

'And Sunderland were real box office. If the League title were settled on crowd appeal we would have run away with it. But we never won anything. We were a team of prima donnas, twelve stars for eleven places. I played between Ivor Broadis and Shackleton but we never really hit it off. We were never all pals together. If two of us were talking to each other, then the other was left out, and similarly if Ivor and Len were "thick" then it would be my turn for the freeze treatment.'

Ford's first appearance in Sunderland's colours was against Chelsea at Stamford Bridge but such was the vigilance of John Harris, the Londoner's centre-half, that he was blotted out and the Roker men lost 3–0. 'The sooner someone else becomes the costliest player in football, the better I shall like it,' said Ford afterwards.

But his first game at Roker was a triumph, for he notched three of the five goals by which Sunderland beat Sheffield Wednesday. That first season in the north he scored 16 goals in 26 League games and his next two years were his most productive in the game, when he topped 20 on both occasions. When both Wales and Sunderland wanted him for a continental tour after the 1953 campaign, Ford did an extraordinary shuttle between the two. First he played for Wales v France in Paris, two days later he helped his club at Malmo, Sweden, then it was back to Belgrade for a cap against Yugoslavia followed by a swift dash to Copenhagen where Sunderland were engaged against a Danish club side.

At last, Wales reclaimed her firebrand. And this time, in November 1953, it was Cardiff who secured Ford's services while another £30,000 changed hands. Whereas he had been one of a galaxy at Roker, the star role was his for the asking at Ninian Park, since the Cardiff policy was to foster local talent where possible, although they recognised that the youngsters needed a lead and that Ford was the man to give it to them.

Ford had already played in 30 internationals, missing three more through injury, and at 29 he was at his peak. When he trotted through the tunnel for his home debut against Middlesbrough a roar swelled round the ground followed by thousands of Welsh voices singing 'We'll keep a welcome in the hillsides'. And Ford's answer to that welcome was to score the only and decisive goal.

But Cardiff wanted more of him than just a marksman. They wanted to use him as a decoy, sacrificing his chance of scoring goals to make them for others, and as such he became a centre-forward very much in the modern idiom. For seven games his goal tally in League, Cup and home international matches stood on 199. Then, playing against Charlton, he went up for a corner, beat Derek Ufton in the air and firmly headed the ball into the net for his 200th and third goal for his new club.

Ford, in fact, only scored those three goals in 20 League outings for Cardiff but next season he was on the rampage again and it was a very perplexed player who heard the news when he went to re-sign that he would, like the other professionals, be put on a sliding scale of wages which meant dropping from £15 to £13 a week if he were relegated to the reserves. Ford rebelled, Cardiff stopped his wages and it was not until three days before the opening of the new season that peace was declared and his back money made up to him.

The rift was healed and Ford buckled to his task again until the November when there came the biggest bombshell of all. Ford was dropped for the first time though he remained the first choice centre-forward for his country. If that drove a wedge between club and player it was widened by the decision of manager Trevor Morris to recall him at inside-left for the match against Birmingham in November.

Ford was quite content to play in the reserves, providing he was at centre-forward, but he did not intend to take a position he had never held, an objection which may seem strange in these days of fluid football and pseudo centre-forwards. But despite the change of emphasis in his play for Cardiff, which he had been glad enough to carry out, Ford felt sincerely that his future was bound up in wearing a number nine shirt, and argued that though he had played inside-right to Charles in the Welsh side it was merely to form a double spearhead.

Ford regarded himself as a specialist and as such he was not prepared to give up his star value by playing in a strange position any more than one would expect to see Norman Wisdom cast as Hamlet, however well he might perform that role. Cardiff saw Ford's reaction as a threat to club discipline and promptly announced that he had been suspended for 14 days and put on the transfer list.

While he was banned from the ground, Ford spent the time selling paint brushes as clubs once more queued for his signature. Even Headington of the Southern League joined in, claiming that they could raise a fee of £15,000 and pay Ford £25 a week, which was more than the League maximum. It was the first time that a club outside the Football League had joined in the bidding for an international when still at the height of his career.

His suspension over, Ford returned to the Cardiff fold at centre-forward for the reserves, at the same time that the first team were, ironically, opposing his old club, Sunderland. Again the storm blew itself out and both club and player weathered it.

Ford was restored to the first team against Wolves and his goal gave Cardiff the shock win of the day, for they were the first team to win a League fixture at Molineux in a year.

When the club's international back, Alf Sherwood, was injured Ford took over the captaincy and in five weeks inspired his side to drive away their relegation worries. The new responsibilities seemed to give Ford a fresh incentive and Cardiff appointed him as captain for the next season. However by November there came a double blow; he was dropped both by his club and his country and when demoted to the reserves Ford said that he wanted to quit, and that he had no intention of finishing on soccer's rubbish heap.

Ford's loss of form coincided with the publication of a book he had written and also with revelations made in newspaper articles – revelations which apparently led to a League suspension *sine die* for alleged refusal to substantiate reports of irregularities.

The decision caused a bitter debate on the rights of the League to deprive a man of his livelihood because the sentence had been imposed not for anything he had done on the field or in dealings with his club but for the exposure of practices which, in his view, marred the game which was his life. So, ever a fighter, Ford went before a three-man F.A. appeals board who rescinded the ban on him. They ruled that he had committed no offence under Football League regulations though they expressed their disapproval of the allegations he had made against unnamed clubs and players without apparently offering any proof as to their accuracy.

Four months later however, in July 1957, the Football Association did react strongly as part of their findings when they inquired into the affairs of Sunderland, an investigation which followed some of the disclosures Ford had made.

By that time, however, Ford had signed for PSV, Eindhoven, who had agreed to pay Cardiff a fee in excess of £5,000 without even seeing him play. And when Ford scored four goals on his first appearance for them they congratulated themselves on their business acumen. In fact, Ford went on a scoring spree in Holland and his 51 goals in 54 games in the 1958 season were a major factor in his club finishing runners-up to Ajax in the championship.

In December, 1959, and after more than two years in Holland, Ford was told that he was crippled for life and would never play serious soccer again. Four times in eight months he had been under treatment from the surgeons for an ankle injury, and now they considered the damage so serious that a further operation would not be of any benefit. Ford shrugged the news off like he would brush an imaginary speck of dirt from his immaculate suits.

It was a staggering blow, not only for Ford but for the Dutch because his behaviour in Holland had been beyond reproach and he had proved a tremendous crowd-puller. When he had played in a pre-season friendly for P.S.V. against visiting Sheffield United he had shown that his ability to puncture defences and grab goals had been unimpaired and the unanimous Sheffield verdict was that, at 36, he would still be a menace in League football.

Ford's reaction to the verdict of the medicos was typical of the man. He vowed to return to soccer, and more, to rejoin the League fray, for despite the friendliness of the Dutch and the pleasant conditions at Eindhoven he was tired of his exile and wanted to return to his native Wales.

In February he was back at Ninian Park, sitting in the directors' box as a guest of the visiting Brighton manager, Bill Lane, and when spectators in the stand recognised him they rose to cheer. When he was asked about his ankle, Ford said simply: 'It has made a miraculous recovery. I have seen a specialist and he is very optimistic. In fact, I have already had a kick-about.'

It was Newport County who pricked their ears at the news. Although struggling along on a shoestring budget, they scraped together the £2,000 P.S.V. wanted for his transfer but the Dutch club sportingly agreed that the fee should not be handed over until the League had decided to re-instate Ford and confirm his registration.

After a summer's rest Ford was ready to boomerang. Despite the fact that he could not wear a football boot until little more than a week before his comeback he promised not only to restore the fortunes of Newport – 'a great little club which has not had half the success it deserves' he said – but regain his place in the Welsh side.

Ford's spirit and optimism were untamed. His one note of caution came when he begged fans not to expect too much of him too soon. He reckoned on possibly five more years in League football and even agreed to play at inside-left. 'I have not joined Newport as a crowd-pulling gimmick,' he said, 'they will have their money's worth out of me.'

Unhappily, a struggling side is not the best medium for rehabilitation and Ford's three goals in eight appearances worked out at something approaching £670 a goal. Since it was going to take him longer than he expected to capture his old flair, Newport suggested a spell in the reserves. But the thought of finishing in the Welsh League was too much of a blow to Ford's pride and he told the club that unless he could be guaranteed a first team place he would like a move, whereupon his contract was torn up by mutual consent.

Ford saw the 1960-61 season out with Romford in the Southern League. This time the transfer was free. But he did a great job in helping Romford to avoid sliding back from the Premier into the First Division from which they had been promoted in their first term as professionals the previous year. Most of the old dash had gone but Ford still had a shrewd soccer brain and positional sense, and he hovered wherever there was a space waiting for the pass that would give him time to bring his still-lethal shooting into play.

That was the last fans saw of him in competitive play. Romford were satisfied and offered him terms for the following season but when Ford rejected them the club freed him.

After all, Ford was a thorough businessman with several interests outside the game, and it was not his intention to sink into oblivion in minor football after touching the heights with 38 caps, 23 goals for his country and a further 177 in League games.

So Ford settled near Cardiff with his wife, Louise, who was a village beauty queen and whose parents had a hotel in Swansea. One recent Christmastide it was two rugby balls that Trevor took home to his sons, David and Martin.

Soccer? 'I don't care if they play rugby or even ping-pong as long as they are healthy,' replied Trevor simply.

But ask the doctors and they will say that Trevor owes his life to soccer for all the punishment that it meted out to him.

In June 1969, Ford was involved in a serious car crash near Bridgend when his chest was crushed against the steering wheel. It was some time before help reached the stricken player and by then he had not only lost a considerable amount of blood but there was so much fluid in the lungs it was a miracle he did not suffocate. His superb fitness, borne of years of strict training, enabled him to make yet another remarkable recovery.

Since his retirement he has not put on more than two pounds in weight and he is still so slim round the waist that he can wears his son's trousers. On a Sunday morning, the trim Trevor can often be seen in the local enjoying a drink with his neighbour, Tony Lewis, the Glamorgan cricket captain. Just before the war, Ford was offered professional terms with Glamorgan and once he fielded as a volunteer in a county match when the 12th man was already engaged.

Ford still keeps his link with soccer. He writes on the game for the Welsh editions of a Sunday newspaper, having stepped into the post vacated by the former Swansea and Cardiff manager, Trevor Morris, when Morris took over as assistant secretary to the Welsh F.A.

If Swansea had some justification for parting with Ford, they certainly missed out in a big way with John Charles who was playing left-half for his school when they won the local championship and he was watched by Joe Sykes, a scout for the Vetch Field club.

John, and his brother Melvyn, would play soccer with anything they could lay their hands, or feet, on. They would kick a tin can through the streets on the way to school and, even in summer, they would stop out playing in the park until dusk. The game received formal recognition in the family when both lads received a pair of football boots and there was a ball to go with them. But, sad to relate, the ball lasted only a day before it was squashed beyond repair by a passing lorry.

When John joined the Swansea groundstaff on leaving school there was little hint either in his approach or his build of the power he was to become. Still only 15, he had only three games for the 'A' side in his first season and none at all in the next one. He helped to weed and tidy the terraces and the nearest he came to senior soccer was to help care for the players' equipment. His skivvying stint finished for the day, he would go back to the park at Cwmdu and it was there that a Leeds United scout watched him and made a recommendation to his chief, Major Frank Buckley, who had a remarkable perception for spotting talent in its embryo stage. Right away, Buckley said that Charles was the lad who made the difficult things look easy. The skill was inbred, it was just a case of developing it.

Buckley laid the foundations for the incredible versatility of Charles, who was to become one of the great soccer rarities by his ability to play effectively in whatever position he was given. It was one of the first tenets of the Leeds chief that a player should be equally competent with either foot and Charles had played on both flanks when he was quietly blooded in the first team for the last match of the season against the Rovers at Blackburn.

Even then, but for a misunderstanding, Wales might have reclaimed their shooting star. Buckley had earlier sent Charles to Cardiff as twelfth man and told the lad he could go from there to spend a few days at his Swansea home.

The old familiar surroundings made Charles so homesick that he resolved to ask for his release when he returned to Leeds. He began his plea to Buckley by addressing him as mister. The chief preferred to be called 'Major' and having admonished him, patted him on the back and told him to think no more about it, thinking that Charles had gone to see him to thank him for his leave.

As Charles was soon to become a regular first team player the thoughts of moving evaporated, especially as he met a pretty bank clerk, Peggy, at a dance and fell in love with the Leeds girl.

Wales rushed the prodigy into the side to face Ireland at Wrexham as a centre-half but although they forced a goalless draw Charles was a failure and more than two years were to pass before he was given another chance.

Even as a centre-half, and at a period when adventurous pivots were unfashionable, Charles proved a great builder of attacks. He had the speed and strength to go up in support of his forwards, and his supremacy in the air enabled him to command the midfield like a colossus. Then one Spring morning in 1951, Buckley told him that he wanted him to play at centre-forward, shrewdly explaining to the demurring Charles that he would have more chance to show his constructive flair there.

'You know all the tricks of a centre-forward. Now you can use them yourself,' he said. And how well Charles carried out Buckley's plan can be gauged from the fact that in the 1952-53 season he scored 30 goals in 21 matches and next term headed the League marksmen with a club record of 42.

By the time Wales recalled him he was confident of his power and his skills and when they beat Ireland 3–2, he volleyed home one goal, headed another and made the third, forming a dangerous spearhead with Ford. So it was not surprising that when Cardiff dropped Ford in November 1955 they should slap in a £40,000 bid for the Leeds giant.

Charles's reaction to the news was typical of the innate modesty of the man. 'No player is worth that much money,' he said simply. Yet his drawing power was such that he boosted the gates wherever he played and when he turned out at Middlesbrough the attendance was 16,000 above the average at Ayresome Park for a Second Division game.

John had already scored more than 100 goals for Leeds in League football and the first of these when he was still only 17 was probably the most memorable. The score was 1–1 and the Plymouth crowd were whistling for the referee to blow for time when, instead, the official awarded a penalty, a decision that was hooted by the home fans. Charles was ordered to take the kick. He seemed capable of shutting himself off from the bedlam around him, coolly placed the ball on the spot and without fuss or ceremony slammed it past Bill Shortt, the Argyle goalkeeper who was later to join him in the Welsh team.

This was just one of a number of incidents which proved that Charles had the right temperament for the big-time. On another occasion when he was playing centre-forward against Brentford at Leeds the score was 2–2 with only a few minutes left for play. Suddenly Charles, lurking in midfield, received the ball near the halfway line. He had already scored both his side's goals and now he set off on a dazzling run in which he had five defenders sliding the wrong way, calmly drew the goalkeeper off his line and then tapped the ball past him into the net. Tommy Lawton was in the Brentford team that day and he added his congratulations to those showered on Charles by his team-mates.

It was the work of a soccer virtuoso, and examples of his artistry became so common that even the shy, self-effacing Charles, who nevertheless was a man of ambition as anyone of determination must be, realised that his flair deserved a better stage than that provided by Second Division football. So he asked for a transfer.

On the night that the board rejected his request in the autumn of 1955, Leeds were due to play a friendly with Hibernian and the cheers which greeted the decision when it was announced over the loudspeakers prompted one reporter to describe their reaction as being akin to the news of the relief of Mafeking. Charles' own answer was to go out and play a stormer.

But he did far more than that. Raich Carter, one of England's greatest inside forwards who won caps both before and after the war, first with Sunderland and then with Derby County, had taken over as Leeds manager, and he appointed Charles as skipper. Under his guidance Leeds won promotion to the First Division in 1956. Charles had spent part of the previous season bolstering the defence but now he went up front again with the result that he topped the division's scorers with 38 goals.

Big-spending Sunderland had flashed their cheque book again with an offer of £50,000 and Charles, now in a home of his own, was happy that that was turned down, too. But when, in the Spring of 1957, clubs from Italy and Spain began an auction for his services, with offers that no British club could match, it soon became apparent that Charles would be lost to home football.

As a 17-year-old tea boy, he had accepted a £10 signing-on fee as though it was a fortune. Now he was offered £10,000 to join Juventus, of Turin, plus a salary of £100 a month with bonuses up to £25 a time for a win away from home. There were other perks such as a large flat, furniture, a car and perhaps, not least, a primer so that he could learn Italian! For Leeds, there was a fee which has been variously quoted but by common consent cannot have been much less than £65,000, which made Charles easily the most expensive British player at that time.

Although not the pioneer of moves to the continent, Charles, by his later success in Italy, undoubtedly popularised such transactions. Great players like Denis Law and Jimmy Greaves followed his example and though at the time their absence seemed an irreparable loss to the League, their departure led to closer British interest in continental methods and an exchange of ideas which laid the foundation for the technical revolution that was to come.

Much of our league play was too fast for subtleties. The theme was one more of hustle and bustle. Charles found the pace of Italian football slower and while the marking was closer so, too, was the support. With his build and skill, Charles soon became adept at screening the ball and winning it by positional interceptions rather than a direct challenge. He found that Italian football was often a matter of hugs and kisses and when he scored a goal he could expect to be dragged to the ground and nearly suffocated.

The Italians played first not to lose rather than to win and developed defensive formations which were not so highly organised in this country until Sir Alf Ramsey began planning for our successful assault on the World Cup in 1966. But the greatness of Charles was that he could shine at the back and also take on the curtain stretched in front of his opponent's goal with minimal support and a fair chance of success. In addition his unruffled temperament was just what was needed to calm his more excitable companions, and under his influence, they played with a new poise and confidence. It would not be correct to say that Charles was a great centre-forward in Italy because the statement would not be complete. He was great in whatever position he had to fill but, through the system, Italian fans had been starved of the essence of football – goals – and that's what Charles gave back to them. When he scored three goals against Lazio, of Rome, Italian commentators said they could find no parallel with him.

When Charles left Leeds he gave them a grand climax with two goals in 18 minutes against Sunderland. When he began with Juventus he laid the foundation for his future successes with ten goals in five matches on their pre-season tour of Sweden. They had negotiated for him under the shadow of relegation and the knowledge that if they did not keep their place they would not be able to keep him, since foreign players were not permitted in the second division. Yet, with the acquisition of Charles and the Argentinian ball juggler, Enrique Sivori, they swept to the championship. Charles did not miss a game and with 29 goals and three hat-tricks he was top scorer in Italian football and voted the country's player of the year.

While Charles was with Juventus they won the league three times and the cup twice. When they emulated Spurs by doing the double in their country Juventus achieved a record 55 points with 92 goals of which Charles's share was 23. There were sterling deeds for Wales, too, as he played centre-forward in the World Cup team that drew with Hungary, Mexico and Sweden, before beating Hungary 2–1 in a play-off in 1958. But he was so clobbered on the way that he missed the quarter-final with Brazil and Wales went down 1–0.

By the beginning of 1962, Charles was hankering to return to England. He had expressed such thoughts much earlier but had been determined to honour his contracts with the Italians and build up the financial security which had been beyond his scope as a League player in England. Despite the fact that he had had a serious knee operation and was now past 30, Juventus were so keen to keep him that they offered him £18,000 for one season. Such was the measure of his fame in Italy.

But Charles thought that he was near the end of his span as a forward, or at least an Italian-style attacker, where the numerical odds were so highly stacked against the individuals up front and where obstruction and body checking and sly, but equally dangerous, measures were the vogue more than the direct tackling experienced at home.

During Charles's five-year absence in Italy, Leeds had slipped back into the Second Division and looked at one time to be heading for the Third, so it was a tremendous effort on their part to raise the £50,000-plus that Juventus demanded for his release. The irony came when he reappeared at Elland Road, for many fans, incensed at the raised admission charges, boycotted the game and only 14,199 turned up to salute their erstwhile conquering hero.

Within two months of his return, there was talk of Charles returning to Italy, for he could neither resettle in Leeds or adjust himself to the quicker pace of English football. He was now much heavier and a back injury did not help him to ease his way into his old sphere. The persistent requests of Charles for a return to the sunnier, and in some respects, less exacting climes of Italy eventually wore down the resistance of the Leeds directors so that, after just three months with the Yorkshire club, he was transferred to Roma while another £70,000 changed hands and the £8,000 home bought for him at Wetherby with its three garages, central heating and terraced lawns, was put up for sale.

This time, Charles made another blistering start with a fine goal which had the Roma fans delirious with joy, but the happiness of the Italian reunion was almost as fleeting as that in Leeds had been and within three months Charles was dropped for the first time in his continental career.

Wherever Charles went in Italy, he was preceded by clarion calls and ballyhoo. Great things were expected of a great player and it was anticipated that he would churn out the goods all the time like a machine making liquorice allsorts. When Charles slipped off his own lofty pinnacle then the criticism was as barbed as the praise had been vociferous, and the harsh way in which he was rejected first by Leeds supporters and then by Roma must have had a serious undermining effect on such a sensitive character.

At last, Charles returned to Wales. Cardiff clinched his transfer, this time for only £20,000, but, plagued by injuries, he was reduced to reserve football to gain fitness and form.

Undoubtedly his finest hour for Cardiff came when he piloted them to a momentous victory over Sporting Lisbon in the European Cup Winners' Cup in December 1964. Even the most fervent Welsh supporters could not see how their side, struggling at the wrong end of the Second Division, were going to overthrow a team that the previous season had whipped Manchester United 5–0.

In Lisbon, Charles was given the role as sweeper, an extra bulwark between the goalkeeper and a line of defenders. It was the first time he had taken up such a position but he accepted the challenge joyfully, remembering the many occasions in Italy when he had been confronted with a similar formation. Charles had plaster protecting four stitches in a head wound and yet such was his courage that he went into every aerial challenge without flinching. As Sporting Lisbon set up wave upon wave of attack, Charles was the rock on which they crashed and, with two goals from breakaways, Cardiff triumphed against all the odds by 2–1.

By holding on to their precious lead in the second leg when Charles adopted a similar defensive role, Cardiff qualified for a tie against Zaragoza, of Spain, and ironically it was an error by Charles, who had looked like a giant against pygmies, that ended their run.

After a 2–2 draw in the first leg, Cardiff held on at Ninian Park until the 74th minute when Canario, the former Real Madrid right winger, feinted to pass to his right-half who came up on the outside and sent John the wrong way. As John moved out to intercept the expected pass, so Canario swept on through the gap for the decisive goal. For the last 16 minutes, Charles was up at centre-forward again while Cardiff hopefully punted long balls into the penalty area. But the chains round Charles now were too closely linked and the watchful Spaniards gave him no chance to retrieve his blunder.

At the end of the 1965 season Cardiff told Charles that he would have to accept a cut in wages. The news had several clubs hopefully queueing for his signature and Cardiff even agreed another five-figure fee with Bournemouth but Charles said that he would not uproot his family again, and then informed Cardiff that as he could not accept their terms he had decided to work outside football.

Charles buckled down to a scrap metal business with his brother, Mel, who had been at Cardiff with him – the only time the brothers were with the same club – but within days he had reached an agreement to carry on playing at Ninian Park. Perhaps that was a mistake for he played only eight League games, one of those as a substitute, scored four first team goals and was hampered by another knee injury which required an operation. Thus at the end of the season, the Gentle Giant who had cost more than £200,000 in transfer fees, was given a free move. In a first class career spanning 18 years, he had scored 269 League goals and won 38 caps.

Charles was snapped up by ambitious Hereford United where he not only delighted his new club but every Southern League ground he visited. When he turned out at Nuneaton, for example, the takings were £700 – the highest for the club in eleven years.

Charles really made things bubble in the cider apple kingdom. He admitted that he still 'got a hell of a kick out of scoring goals' and there were plenty of kicks with 25 in his first 24 games. At 35, he was now strictly conservative, nursing his wind and his strength, and saying that pacing was the art of a long football life. Some supporters complained that he would often run farther and faster to apologise to a player for bowling him over than he would to collect a loose ball, but if the mildness of the man showed through, so, too, did the power, and the chances he ignored were forgiven in the light of the many that he snapped up.

Charles became such a success with Hereford that at least one Football League club tried to woo him back again but in December 1967, Hereford gave him an early Christmas present by making him manager, and, if Charles has his way, he will still renew his connection with the Football League without changing his job.

Now he commutes regularly between his home at Cardiff where he runs a sports shop, and Hereford, the club he is determined to pilot to higher status.

Charles was the complete player. Trevor Ford, who has touched greatness himself and can appreciate it, says he was a genius. Perhaps he burst upon the soccer scene too soon, for all-round versatility has been more in vogue in recent seasons than when he was at his peak. Centre-half or centre-forward . . . what did Charles prefer himself?

Let Charles answer for himself: 'Whether I liked centre-forward best depended upon whether I was scoring goals. If you are on the target, then there is no position to touch it. But if you are not, then I would sooner be a centre-half. The spotlight doesn't dazzle you quite so much there.

'It is all rather mercurial,' he went on. 'You go three or four games without scoring and you feel as though the world

DERЕK DOUGAN . . . 'has the power by his presence alone to put a few more thousands on the gate'

JEFF ASTLE . . . 'his powerful headwork reminiscent of giants of the past'

PETER OSGOOD . . . 'Old-timers compared him with David Jack and moderns with Jimmy Greaves'

JOE ROYLE . . . 'His industry not only sharpened his skills but steeled his resolve'

is falling in on top of you. Then you score the vital one in a one-nothing victory and you're back on top again. One thing I do know, centre-forward is the most glamorous position in the game and it is coming back. More and more teams are pinning their faith on having a big man up front in a number nine shirt.'

8
Dougan: The Irish Showman

The man who dared, became the man who cared. That in a nutshell sums up the turbulent career of the exciting, exasperating but invariably intensely invigorating Derek Dougan, the pride of Ireland, although numbering among his many nicknames that of 'the Irish scamp'.

In some 13 years of League football, Dougan has proved himself more than one of the best of the contemporary centre-forwards. He has also been one of the game's great entertainers. He claims that it is the players' job to give the fans their money's worth and no one can ever accuse him of failing in that aim. At a time when the real personalities in our top sports are being submerged by increasing pressures and tensions, extroverts like Dougan are as rare as roses in December.

Scowls and snarls are the badges of modern soccer. Smiles are signs of softness and lack of dedication. But Dougan, although he has matured and mellowed since his early jesting days, can still be depended upon to extract the maximum drama or humour out of any situation and because of that has the power by his presence alone to put a few more thousands on the gate.

Often in trouble with authority, Dougan has now succeeded so well as a lucid diplomat that he is chairman of the Professional Footballers' Association, has even championed the cause of referees, and made a tremendous impact as a sports commentator on television both during the last World Cup and since.

Dougan was the second of six children and the first boy born to a Belfast family whose head was a shipyard worker and it seemed that he was destined to become an electrician. He was such a sensitive lad that few could guess that he would make the sparks fly in the high-tension atmosphere of League football.

His passion for the game began early enough, when he was eight, and by the time he was 14 he had won his first cap as a schoolboy international. He also gained honours with Ireland's youth, junior and amateur sides and while with Distillery he played inside forward, outside-left, left-half and centre-half. Left-half was his favourite position and even when Eddie Lever, then Portsmouth manager, pipped Raich Carter of Leeds for his signature in October 1957 there was no hint that he would become a great centre-forward. As with several others, the transformation came about by sheer accident, in his case several accidents. Plagued by a long injury list, Portsmouth thrust him in for his League debut for their toughest engagement of the season – away to the champions, Manchester United. One of the Pompey casualties was their England leader, Ray Crawford, and so Dougan was in although, as he observed laconically much later: 'They tried six others before they tossed the number nine shirt to me.'

Straight from playing a major part in a shock win, Dougan was called up for Ireland's B side to face the Rumanians against whom he notched a glittering hat-trick. His early form prompted Sir Stanley Matthews to comment that he was the centre-forward sensation of his age. He predicted, correctly, that with his height and weight – and at 6 feet 3 inches Dougan had at least an inch or two advantage over most centre-halves he met – he would be a terror to opposing goalkeepers.

But after that electrifying start there were times when the lean and languid Dougan fused. Essentially an individualist, his form was as variable as a woman's hemline. A tricky and confident dribbler, he believed in holding the ball. With his exceptional control he could beat a man and yet there were times when he ran into trouble while his colleagues waited for him to do something constructive.

At the same time, Dougan became one of soccer's showmen by accident. He rolled over several times after a fall and the Fratton Park crowd roared with laughter. So Dougan seemed to decide that if they liked acrobatics he would provide them, and he added such gimmicks as leading the applause for his own goals, throwing up his arms in triumph, bowing, and staring down on small referees. If that official was very short then Dougan would advance as near as he dared so that the crowd had the full treatment of the disparity in height. He also became a master of the aggrieved 'Who me?' look and the comical gesture of despair when pulled up by the referee. Boos and jeers stimulated rather than upset this remarkable character while the reaction of the fans to his expertise and histrionics varied according to loyalties. While the faithful cheered and grinned, the enemy' dubbed him a show-off and a clown.

For two years the Irishman built up his reputation as Dougan the Dazzler at Portsmouth but when Lever was followed as manager by Freddie Cox things began to go wrong for him. He was accused of being unpredictable, to which his reply was that centre-forward was not his position anyway, and in March 1959 he was sold to Blackburn for £11,000 which was £7,000 more than Pompey had paid for him when they bought him from Ireland.

The following season he scored 16 goals in 42 League and Cup games including two great goals in the semi-final against Sheffield Wednesday which put Rovers in their first Final since 1928.

That was not bad going for a man who even now regards himself than no more than a makeshift leader, but of more than 200 goals he has scored in top class football one of his earliest gave him as much pleasure as any. That was when he was still with Portsmouth and he recalls it vividly because, as still a raw teenager, he was confronted by Billy Wright of Wolves and had to beat him first to gain a clear sight of the goal.

Now Blackburn were in their first final since 1928 and Wolves were the opponents. And Dougan was so anxious to play that he concealed a leg injury. True, he had a midweek fitness test but his examiners were so intent on his running that they did not realise the effort it cost him or spot the pain that showed on his face. So Dougan turned out at Wembley, the tallest man on the field, but his height was not enough. He was blotted out of the game by Bill Slater and soon realised that the demanding Wembley pitch is no place for a man recovering from a pulled muscle, as Blackburn slumped to a 3–0 defeat.

The eclipse of Dougan would have been one of the after-match talking points if he had not been the centre of a far bigger sensation, for the news leaked out that he had asked for a transfer. Derek was not happy with the Rovers' set-up and he posted his transfer request to the then manager, Dally

Duncan, on the morning of the Final after six verbal requests had gone unanswered. Dougan timed his appeal so that it would reach official quarters on the Monday but somehow the news had leaked out almost before the Final was over.

Dougan later withdrew his request and Duncan departed from the Rovers before he did, but when the new chief, Jack Marshall, promoted Fred Pickering, then a reserve full-back, to take his place he again asked for a move. Dissatisfied with the terms he had been offered for the following season he even flew to the Continent on his own initiative in a bid to fix up with a Belgian club.

In July 1961, this impetuous giant was transferred to Aston Villa for a fee which has been variously quoted as being between £12,000 and £20,000. This was his third club in four years and Villa needed him to replace English international Gerry Hitchens, who had joined Inter-Milan.

But after joining in Villa's League Cup Final celebrations to mark their win over Rotherham, Dougan was involved in a car crash on the way home. A broken arm and a head so severely gashed that 20 stitches were needed put him out of football for three months.

So anxious was Dougan to make his presence felt at Villa that weeks before doctors thought he should be kicking a ball, let alone heading one, he was pleading with manager Joe Mercer to be put in the League side. He had had two hard games in the reserves and it seemed that Dougan was on the way back when a severe wintry period brought soccer to a halt for a while. During the period of slip and slide, another blow befell Dougan. Falling in the street, he twisted a knee so badly that when the ice eased its grip he was not ready to seize his chance .

It is never easy returning to a struggling side, as Villa were then, and Dougan found that several changes had been made – the purchase of Phil Woosnam from West Ham was one – to which he could not readily adapt himself.

The unpredictable topsy-turvy nature of a player's career was never better illustrated than by events for Dougan in that Autumn of 1962. Recalled by Ireland after being overlooked for a series of internationals, he was the hero of their shock 2–0 win over Poland in the European Nations Cup and it was taken for granted that he would lead the line against England.

But then came Villa's match against Nottingham Forest. As Ron Wylie challenged the Forest goalkeeper, Peter Grummitt, the ball ran loose and Dougan instinctively jabbed out a foot and tried to hook the ball round the falling 'keeper. Dougan was sent off the field for allegedly kicking an opponent and, though Grummitt spoke up in his defence, he was suspended for 14 days. Thus Dougan had the unenviable record of becoming the first man to miss a chance of playing against England through a suspension which, he reckons, cost him £200. There were long arguments on the ethics of the F.A. decision, arrived at by Englishmen, who robbed Ireland of one of their leading stars against England, but the upshot was that Dougan had to watch from the stands as his side went down in what was, he recalls, one of the most frustrating afternoons of his life.

During his stay in Birmingham, Dougan fell in love with a German girl, Jutta Fichtl, who had come to this country to improve her English. She was only 20 when she said 'yes' to his proposal of marriage but her parents objected on the grounds that not only was she too young but she could not cope with the problems of living in a strange country. Their decision was certainly a contributory factor to Dougan losing much of his sparkle and in May 1963 he was put on the transfer list.

Dougan had known within a month of meeting Jutta in a restaurant that she was the girl for him and, without waiting to find out what was happening to his career, he flew to Munich where she had returned.

Several clubs made enquiries for him, among them Third Division Peterborough whose manager, Jack Fairbrother, was informed that if he could find Dougan he could buy him. Fairbrother traced him through the help of the German Embassy and his arrival on the continent coincided with the news that Jutta's parents had approved of Derek, their engagement being announced when they returned to Birmingham.

Dougan said at the time that Jutta's parents did not regard him as a footballer but as a human being, and that made a new angle! Despite the fact that he was stepping down two divisions, his value increased once more, Peterborough paying a fee in excess of £20,000, but Dougan said he was convinced he was doing the right thing and the club had such progressive ideas that he was sure they were booked for promotion.

Peterborough bought a man who was no longer a brash, rash kick-and-hope individualist. Perhaps his marriage that July of 1963 accelerated his development but the fact remains that he became rather less of an exhibitionist and rather more of a team man. Another spur to his responsibility was his appointment as team captain. Not that Dougan would ever be content to be one of the crowd. At Villa Park he had been nicknamed 'Cheyenne' because he had had his head shaved, but even if this was a showman's gimmick Dougan had a reason for it. He thought it would strengthen the growth as he was going a little thin on top. And anyway he wanted to feel fresh for a new season!

His passion for sleek, fast cars, elegant suits and good cigars remained. His new nickname was 'Mr Posh', the name frequently ascribed to his club.

Fairbrother was soon concerned for the safety of his new star for he stated bluntly that when Third Division defenders met a player of Dougan's class they made it a priority to put him out of action as quickly as they could.

Dougan has always been a willing subject for being caught up in the emotion and passion of the game. As such he is excitable and unpredictable. He admits that he is a different man on the field from off it. He becomes 'lost' in the ebb and flow of the game, and although he admits, like most stars, that he loves playing before really big crowds – something he missed at Peterborough – he is as impervious to their cheers as to their jeers. In fact, there have been times when boos have stimulated rather than worried him. For all the rough treatment he has endured from defenders, it is surprising that with his volatile ways he has not been guilty of many more misdemeanours himself. He has never set out to destroy opposing defences other than by fair means. There is nothing of the sly, deliberate trickster in Dougan; rather his offences, such as there have been, are open and impulsive.

Once, on the only occasion he played under the guidance of Sir Alf Ramsey for the Rest of Britain side meeting Wales at Cardiff, the England chief told him that with his spirit he could really give the opposing centre-half the runaround. Those few words made Dougan feel good and inspired him to play a blinder.

Dougan began with a bang at Peterborough with 13 goals in his first 18 League matches although only one of them came away from home. But his Third Division 'exile' cost him his international place and he was so closely shadowed that he lost his effectiveness and was dropped by the club, an incident which caused a local sensation since he was Peterborough's highest paid player.

Back came Dougan like a boomerang to put himself at the top of the F.A. Cup marksmen with hat-tricks against Salisbury in the first round and Chesterfield in the third. The reward for Peterborough was a glittering home tie against Arsenal. The wealthy from the marble halls of Highbury came that fateful February afternoon in 1965 to put the upstarts of the Fens in their place.

John Radford scored the goal that Arsenal had long threatened a minute from the interval and the Londoners began the second half with such assurance that the rest of the game seemed no more than a formality. They had reckoned without the explosive Dougan.

With just 17 minutes left, Dougan, with Ure at his shoulder on the edge of the penalty area, checked his stride just long enough to send the Arsenal pivot the wrong way, and then lashed a first-time shot into the net.

All Peterborough erupted. Dougan had really set light to the fuse and with just a few minutes remaining their irresistible surge carried them through the Arsenal ranks again for Peter McNamee to slot in the winner.

Altogether Dougan notched 28 goals that season but despite their successful Cup run – they were eventually beaten by Chelsea in the sixth round – Peterborough were still in debt and, in an economy campaign, Dougan's terms were reduced. Then Leicester made an offer approaching £25,000 for him and Derek prepared for his return to the First Division. He did so on the sands of the Costa Del Sol where daily he ran three miles before breakfast, played soccer with the Spanish boys and then trained with a local club in the evening.

It was the following October, when Ireland recalled him for

his first cap for three years, that he scored the goal which has given him as much pleasure as any.

The Scots had taken the lead with a header by Alan Gilzean, so now let Dougan himself take up the story: 'I was partnering George Best that day at Windsor Park, working a double spearhead with Willie Irving. George worked into the Scot's penalty area with that wonderful control of his when he was blatantly fouled. I threw up my arms in appeal for a penalty when I noticed the ball coming loose to me. So I whacked it with my right foot. I call that my swinger. It thudded against the underside of the bar and dropped into the net.'

That goal set Ireland on the way to a 3–2 victory and when Dougan began at Leicester he had never played so well. Perhaps the influence of the four-leaf clover sent to him by his father and kept in an envelope in his shorts had something to do with it. Dougan had seven goals in his first six matches and the pace scarcely slackened as he finished the season with more than 30. Throughout his stay, Dougan gained more and more admirers. Leicester were frequently congratulated on their bargain in having a man rated as the best centre-forward in Britain.

Yet for all Leicester's potential they never really clicked and in March 1967 manager Matt Gillies informed him that Wolves had made an offer for him which the club had accepted. Again Dougan was Leicester's leading marksman at the time of his transfer with 21 more goals and once more his value leapt – this time to £45,000. Very few players can equal Dougan's record of having enhanced his value with every move.

Dougan's own comment on it was: 'A friend told me that I'm like an antique. I become more priceless with age. I don't know whether that is a compliment or not!'

For all his considerable experience in League football Dougan was only now 28. He was at the peak of his powers and certain that his first experience of Second Division football would not be a long one as Wolves were pressing for promotion.

That aim was duly achieved so that by the start of the 1967-68 campaign Dougan was back in the top flight where he has remained ever since. But once again he had to overcome a lean spell that brought only two goals in three months and there was more trouble with referees as he took the risks which are all part of a goal-hungry player's trade.

If Wolves wanted Dougan, there is no doubt that Dougan needed Wolves. At last he found a club where he fitted in both on and off the field, and one where his full talents could be harnessed to the advantage of the side. Manager Bill McGarry has shown a happy knack for bringing the best out of his squad and Dougan has proved no exception.

Yet he needed all the club's understanding and support, for when the F.A. introduced their suspended sentence scheme for offenders at the beginning of the 1969 season, Dougan had the dubious privilege of being one of the first to be dealt with under it. 'I'm an F.A. guinea-pig,' he said at the time.

Dougan had received a deferred two-week suspension for allegedly kicking Peter Eustace, of Sheffield Wednesday. He played under the shadow of knowing that any further misdemeanour would bring the sharpest retribution. He knew also that the more unscrupulous of his opponents would play on this fear. He was an obvious target for provocation. No wonder Dougan once made a plea for two referees – one to watch the play and the other the players.

Yet ironically when the blow fell it was not for any physical contact but for a few ill-chosen words to the referee which brought him marching orders for the third time in his career. The pity was that two of them had come within seven weeks of each other and the sentence of the F.A. this time was an eight-week ban which meant that he could not play again in 1969. To that point, it was the stiffest sentence imposed on a player for a field occurrence since the war.

During his period of enforced inactivity Dougan redoubled his efforts to raise money for the Mental Health Research Fund, a laudable project in which the club gave him every assistance. In 18 months he had raised £8,000 and now he set out to find £1,500 to provide a motor coach for mentally handicapped children. This was his way of saying thank you for his own two bonny sons, and the money was soon forthcoming.

Mention Dougan's charity work anywhere, and all those who have been connected with it pay tribute to his imaginative approach, gentlemanly charm and obvious sincerity. Few players are endowed with such a heart-warming personality as Derek.

By the time Dougan was ready for his comeback he had another worry, for his three-year-old son Nicholas, had gone down with measles, and Derek could not remember whether he had had it! Thrusting that concern into the background, he had played only three more games when he went up in an aerial duel with Keith Newton, the Everton and England back, and the clash of heads left him with an injured cheekbone.

During his colourful career, Dougan has served under 20 managers and played more than 30 times for his country but in 1970 more doors were opened up to him and he won more hearts with that Irish wit and charm of his than ever before.

Dougan made a tremendous impact with his knowledge and perception when he was chosen by London Weekend TV to be one of their panel of experts to comment on the World Cup. Why Dougan?

The choice was that of the company's sports chief, Jimmy Hill, in conjunction with his executive producer, John Bromley, and Hill explains: 'Over a season we show many interviews with footballers and you obviously register those who have the ability to express themselves, have a personality which bubbles, and some humour which is important. And Dougan combined all three attributes.'

To these he can now add that of being a diplomat for in August 1970 he became the third Irishman to be appointed chairman of the Professional Footballers Association, succeeding Terry Neill and Noel Cantwell. It is doubtful whether the players could have chosen a more devoted advocate, for Dougan cares passionately about his beliefs.

Dougan does not see his future in soccer management but he is very keen on administration and communication and, as an avid reader, it is not surprising that he is now turning his considerable talents to commercial writing.

One of soccer's vintage characters – that's Derek Dougan, and all the signs are that when the time comes for him to hang up his boots, and that could be some while yet, he will still remain in the public eye.

9
Astle, Osgood, Royle: The Modern Look

Whatever the soccer pundits care to call the centre-forwards of today there is no doubt that for the man committed to the goalmouth the game is tough and relentless. The penalty area is the business part of the pitch. It is so crucial that sides willingly surrender the space beyond in order better to control events where they matter most.

The men up front have to be saintly in temperament and fearless in their approach. If a defender succeeds early on in intimidating a striker then his task for the rest of the afternoon is that much easier. The modern player is far more adept at shielding the ball with his body than his predecessors and this tactic invites the tackle from behind by exasperated defenders.

For some time English football has threatened to be submerged in a maze of patterns and formations with set-pieces for every conceivable situation. Each one has its counter and the result is stalemate, a series of predictable moves, many of them snuffed at source. Where the stereotyped is the fashion, then a man with the skill, industry and flair to go it alone and achieve the unexpected is beyond price. Fortunately, for all the increasing tempo and tension of the modern game, such players abound and names such as Allan Clarke, who seems a natural successor to Bobby Charlton in the England side, George Best, whose wizardry has taunted so many sides, and Martin Peters come readily to mind.

Brazil won the World Cup because they had several men, apart from the great Pele, with the individual artistry to throw the best-organised defensive systems into near chaos. And West Germany applied the knock-out blow to England's hopes of retaining the trophy by relying, at the crucial moment, on the individual flair of their substitute, Grabowski, who was prepared to pit his wits and skill against England's defence single-handed if necessary.

But throughout soccer's evolution there is one common thread – a man up front with the strength, power and courage to bang the ball into the net at whatever angle and height it comes to him and however stern the challenge from opponents.

When I spoke to Arsenal manager, Bertie Mee, and congratulated him on the revival at Highbury, he explained the disappearance of the old-type centre-forward by saying: 'It's a question of cutting your suit according to the cloth. For a time we have had a shortage of the big chaps who could play as centre-forwards. Similarly there has been a trend in recent seasons not to have wingers, for the simple reason that the men that match up to the demands of modern play were just not available. This is just a cycle because now we have the big boys beginning to hit the headlines again. We have always been looking for them, but we just have not been able to find them.'

Arsenal, in fact, have two big boys in John Radford and Ray Kennedy, acting as joint spearheads and the need for this doubling up was explained by that shrewd guide of Liverpool, Bill Shankly, who has his own lofty young star in John Toshack.

'There is only one place where you can score goals regularly and that is in the goalmouth,' he said. 'In the old days it used to be one against one, with the centre-half marking the centre-forward and so on. Now, with the modern system, it is three against one, with players expected to funnel back to the areas where possession matters most.

'Positions must vary according to the ebb and flow of the game but I like to keep at least two men up front, and John Toshack is an ideal example of what a striker should be because, apart from his height and his strength, he is good in the air.'

However much styles change, the attributes of a centre-forward, or his counterpart, remain constant. He must not merely be burly, but strong and athletic, and nimble enough to turn and beat an opponent even on those many occasions when he is placed at an immediate disadvantage by receiving the ball when he is facing his own goal rather than the one he is attacking. He must be spring-heeled and fleet of foot, capable of outjumping and outpacing his rivals.

The fortunes of his side so largely depend upon him. The story of the team forced to defend for much of the game and then snatching a goal through the tenacity of their spearhead chasing a clearance down the middle is written somewhere nearly every Saturday afternoon. When goals are at the premium they are at the moment in the top class game, no side can afford the luxury of a marksman who is wayward in his shooting. A heavy load of responsibility rests on his broad shoulders. One goal against the odds can lift a whole team to a performance above that expected of them. One sad miss, perhaps from a solitary chance, can drain confidence and breed despair.

Above all, a centre-forward must be fearless and robust, never shirking a challenge and yet sufficiently unflappable in temperament to shrug aside the shirt-tugging, the barging and the sly and clumsy tackles which are certain to be his lot, and are likely to increase in ratio to his success. The temptation to kick a centre-forward's ankle or shin is very great to the defender who is repeatedly being beaten by him, especially when he knows that if he cannot slow down his rival somehow he will probably receive a roasting from his manager and colleagues when he returns to the dressing room. It is an unfortunate truth that, with pressures what they are, clogging is all part of the game's psychological warfare and it takes a firm and observant referee to stop it. Often punitive action is taken when it is too late.

In three seasons since 1968, the highest individual goal tally in Football League games has been 28, compared with 52 by Terry Bly, when with Peterborough in 1961. Everton won the League title in 1970 with 72 goals – less than two a game and only 12 more than Dixie Dean managed for them in three fewer matches in 1928. In 390 minutes of endeavour in the World Cup in Mexico, England scored four times, a depressing example of how defensive refinements have gradually stifled the game's life blood. If football is to retain its popularity as the Saturday afternoon sports spectacular, then something must be done to alleviate the famine. Several ideas have already been advanced, but the League has consistently shrunk from any reward apart from the marginal one of goal average for scoring feats and in that respect a 1–0 victory ranks more than one achieved by 3–2 or 5–4.

Of the modern marksmen, few have excelled more than Geoff Hurst, whose name became a byword far beyond the ranks of ordinary soccer followers when he scored a hat-trick which was the major factor in England beating West Germany and so winning the World Cup at Wembley in 1966. Often he operated alone, without even the help of conventional wingers, but since then he has always remained at, or close to the top, and the manner in which he has suffered many buffetings without a sign of retaliation is a great tribute to his sporting character.

But to include more on Hurst here would merely add to the confusion of the numbers game, for he does not normally wear the number nine shirt. He may fulfil the same task as a centre-forward but he does not rank as one. So, for leaders closer to the traditional pattern it is necessary to look further afield and there are three especially who have already proved their flair in piercing the defensive armouries.

The first two have a rare feat in common. When West Bromwich won the Cup in 1968, their leader, Jeff Astle, scored in every round and this was repeated two seasons later by Peter Osgood for Chelsea. Both found places in the England World Cup party in Mexico and the third, young Joe Royle, of Everton, looks certain to be challenging strongly for the chief marksman's role when Sir Alf Ramsey comes to sifting his World Cup probables for Munich 1974. Royle proved the powerhouse of Everton's championship-winning effort with 23 of those 72 goals, more than double the total of the club's next most successful marksman, Alan Whittle. All three top six feet and scale more than 13 stone. Royle, indeed, is Astle's tip for the future for he has already stated that if he had to give way to a player it could not be to a better prospect. But what of Astle himself?

This fearless Albion leader has been described as an old-fashioned centre-forward. This stems from his powerful head-work reminiscent of giants of the past such as Dean and Lawton. That is not surprising, for it was Lawton who taught him the timing necessary to add to his natural assets of a keen eye and a strong jump. They linked up while Lawton was manager of Notts County, a club whose name appears with remarkable frequency in this narrative, either as the nursery or near journey's end for the great leaders.

Born at Eastwood, Astle was quick to show his gifts for cracking or nodding the ball past a goalkeeper and after shining as a marksman for West Notts Boys he was snapped up by Notts County where in his first full season he notched 16 goals in 1962–63. In his early days at Meadow Lane, Tony Hateley was also on County's books and he was another who specialised in the high-flying acts, so Jeff was set a good example from the outset.

In September, 1964, Albion stepped in with a successful bid of £25,000 which must rank as one of the bargain buys of that period since in four of the next five seasons Astle scored more goals than anybody else in the team. His value now must be six times that figure.

Since Astle has been at the Hawthorns his club have proved one of the country's best cup-fighting teams. He played in all three of the League Cup finals Albion reached in five seasons, though finishing only once on the winning side when Albion beat West Ham in 1966, the last occasion that the final was staged on a two-legged basis.

The next season he played a major part in guiding the holders to Wembley, scoring in every round, but he failed to find the mark in the final and Albion surrendered the trophy to Queen's Park Rangers by 3–2. Fitting compensation for that setback came a year later when Albion, who share with Newcastle the proud record of having appeared in more finals – ten – than any other club, reached the last stage of the FA Cup and Astle scored the crucial goal that toppled Everton in extra time.

No goal better illustrated Astle's ability to seize on the flicker of a chance. Picking up the ball beyond the Everton penalty area he evaded a tackle and moved forward until he was challenged again. He then tried a right foot shot which cannoned back to him off a defender and in a flash he volleyed it left-footed past Gordon West into the top corner of the net. That score topped a great season for Astle as he headed the scoring list with 35, five more than the target he had set himself, and was voted Midlands player of the year. The honour was well deserved for his feats gave Midlands soccer a lustre it had not enjoyed since the Wolves side under Stan Cullis in the late fifties.

Winning the FA Cup opened the lucrative door to Europe for Albion. Their first venture in the Fairs Cup two years earlier had not lasted long and the pity was that their first continental engagement in the European Cup Winners' Cup was not only a disaster for them but also for soccer as a whole, since it gave rise to some of the most disgraceful scenes ever seen on a football pitch.

Like most stars, Astle discovered that as his fame spread so did the hazards increase. Frequently he has been singled out for 'the treatment' and his temperament has not always withstood the severe strain imposed upon it. As he once admitted, it is difficult not to argue when you know you have been cheated and hard not to hit back when you know you have been the victim of a vicious foul. But Astle could scarcely be blamed for the holocaust which burst over his side on that torrid September evening in Bruges. The trouble began seconds after an Albion shot had hit a post. Astle rushed in and tried to slide the rebound past the diving goalkeeper, an act which the Belgians evidently believed exposed their man to grave risk of injury.

Astle had only done what would have been expected of him in pouncing on the loose ball but suddenly, in a horrifying moment, it seemed as though the whole of the Bruges defence converged on him. As Astle was kicked and punched to the ground so a series of fights developed in the penalty area as colleagues rushed to his assistance. Spectators were aghast at the vicious intensity of the free-for-all as would-be peacemakers among the players were kicked and punched for their pains. Tempers flared to such a flashpoint that armed police had to rush on the field, separating the players with truncheons drawn.

Astle remembers little of what happened. While order was being restored he was carried off on a stretcher and rushed to hospital with severe concussion and a broken bone in his right foot. He recalls refusing a cup of tea at the interval but had no recollection of the goals scored by Bruges before the incident.

If Astle has at times seemed bitter not only at the methods of some of his shadowers, but also the lack of understanding and protection he has experienced with some referees, then that nightmare in Bruges provides justification for his outlook. Once he said that he had been advised that if he were kicked all over the place he should just walk away and count the bruises. 'People who think that way are welcome to try it,' he said.

A third Wembley appearance in successive years appeared out of the question for Astle when Albion lost to Leicester City in the semi-final of the FA Cup but within weeks he was at the stadium again, winning his first full cap and being unlucky not to add his name to the scorers in a 2–1 victory.

His adaptability in strange conditions was proved when he notched two goals against a Mexico eleven on England's South American summer tour in 1969 which was arranged as a scouting mission for the defence of the World Cup. But it did not look as if he would be in the party when he opened the next campaign with a bitter dispute over terms, as Astle pursued his ambition of becoming Albion's first £100 a week basic-wage player. Instead of granting his wish, Albion slapped a heavy fine on him for turning up late at the ground for treatment to a groin injury.

The breach was healed through Astle's loyalty to Albion and the tact and diplomacy of the club manager, Alan Ashman, who did not wish to be at loggerheads with a man he considered to be among the world's most versatile marksmen. Even so, the rift meant that Astle was kept out of the League side for several games and he did not begin his season until well on in September. Three months' later he was back in the England side, replacing Geoff Hurst and helping them to a 1–0 win over Portugal at Wembley.

By the time April came round, Astle had once more achieved his aim of scoring more than 30 goals for his club, a feat recognised by England in his recall for the match against the Scots at Hampden, this time in place of Bobby Charlton.

That game ended in a goalless draw but as the top marksman in the First Division with 91 goals in three seasons Astle was on virtually everyone's list for Mexico and he was certainly on the one that mattered most – Sir Alf Ramsey's. But the World Cup trip was not his happiest period, tremendous experience as it undoubtedly was.

In the war of words that provided an unedifying backcloth to events on the pitch, South American reporters regarded it as part of their business to undermine the confidence of their visitors as far as possible. To this end, some of the England players were held up as subjects for ridicule and Astle's turn for a 'mention in dispatches' came when he had to be helped from a plane in some distress and was promptly accused of being the worse for drink. The truth was that Astle, never the best of air travellers and always nervous about flying, had felt ill during a bumpy journey in which the plane had to battle through tropical storms. The jibes to which he, and other players were subjected, serious as they were, receded into comparative insignificance when the scandal which enveloped the England captain, Bobby Moore, broke. He was alleged to have stolen a £600 bracelet from a jewellery shop and, however contrived and unjust, it was with this cloud of suspicion hanging over them that England had to prepare for their supreme effort.

Astle's big chance of World Cup glory came in the key Group Three match against Brazil after they had just squeezed through against Rumania by Geoff Hurst's goal. With England trailing 1–0, Astle was called on as substitute – and missed a sitter. On one of the rare occasions when England contrived a clear-cut opening on that steamy afternoon in Guadalajara, Astle's normally lethal shooting powers betrayed him. He shot first time and the ball went agonisingly the wrong side of a post.

Back home again, Astle went to South Devon for a holiday and delighted the locals of an inn side when he lent his powerful support to their efforts in a five-a-side tournament which they won with a 5–0 triumph over a Royal Naval College team as the climax. That was a happy interlude after the way he had been pilloried and when he reported to the Hawthorns for training Ashman put him in the reserves so that he could regain his scoring touch.

The Southern League men of Worcester found little wrong with it when Astle raced half the length of the field for a spectacular goal against them. Making him Albion's skipper was the next step, a promotion which evoked from Astle the view that defeat was just that little harder to take now that he was the man in charge on the field. Responsibility sharpens endeavour and Astle was soon back jostling his rivals at the top of the goal charts although his wife, Lorraine, said that the marking of him was so severe it was no longer a pleasure to watch him.

Among so much destruction, Astle is undoubtedly one of the creative elements in the modern game and he has several years yet in which to burnish what is already a bright record. And yet he might have been a cricketer – Notts invited him to have a trial – if Lawton had not called at his home and put him on the groundstaff at Meadow Lane instead of Trent Bridge.

How many vicissitudes in sport can be directly attributed to the vagaries of the British climate? Cricketers accept rain with a stoic resignation built-in by generations of fruitless journeys and pavilion vigils, and soccer, too, has suffered its share of disruption from the three fearful F's – flood, fog and frost. The game is bespattered like raindrops on the windows with examples of chances won and lost through the elements, and Peter Osgood provides one of them.

Osgood was recommended to Queen's Park Rangers for a trial when he was 16. The club acceded to his request but the game in which he was to have been tried was cancelled because the pitch was waterlogged. The question then arose whether the offer should be repeated but another player from the Windsor area, where Osgood was born, expressed the view that he was not worth chasing – some opinion! – and so Rangers kept silent.

Osgood did not rate himself as a professional soccer star. Although he had played representative boys' football for Slough and Berkshire, he was discouraged by the experience of one of his pals, whom he considered a far better player than himself, and who had gone to a League club for a trial and had been rejected. And if Peter wanted to play for anybody, he wanted it to be Arsenal. The Gunners had always been his favourites and they even sent him a trial form, yet Peter, full of self-doubts, threw it away.

The next faltering step for Osgood was a trial at Reading, where he accompanied a pal, but his arrival aroused as much interest as a charlady emptying her bucket down the sink and, with the manager scouting elsewhere, there was no stampede of officials across the pitch to sign him. Thoroughly disillusioned, Peter decided that his soccer would begin and end with his two local sides – Spital Old Boys on a Saturday and the Windsor Corinthians on Sundays.

It was an uncle who played with him for Corinthians who prompted the approach to Chelsea for a trial, which is one reason why 'Ossie' numbers among his nicknames 'the man from Uncle' in addition to the 'wizard of Os'. Chelsea's youth team manager, Dick Foss, gave him the spur he needed by immediately signing him as an amateur.

When he signed as a professional at Stamford Bridge, manager Tommy Docherty's verdict on him was that he was as good as Johnny Byrne – a bustling striker who did yeoman service with several London clubs – on the ground, and as effective as the late Tommy Taylor, of Manchester United, in the air.

Strangely, one of Osgood's earliest senior chances came for England, although he did not win a cap for it. The squad had a full-scale practice game against Chelsea in preparation for the international against Wales in September 1965 and as the chosen centre-forward, Alan Peacock, of Leeds, was required by his club, Osgood was pressed into service to play alongside such men as Jimmy Greaves and the two Bobbies, Charlton and Moore. The gangling Ossie showed his promise by scoring twice and making another in England's 4–3 victory.

Things happened for Osgood in a hurry when he was in his teens. He met his wife, Rosemary, at a town fair on the playing fields of Eton. He was married at 17 and the father of a son a year later. He bought his first car, a small second-hand saloon, and his earnings rose in little more than two years from £8 as a bricklayer helping his father to £80 as a Chelsea first-teamer.

Dave Sexton, who gave up the coaching job at Chelsea to become Leyton Orient manager at that time, described him as a big and clever forward, who was tremendous in the air, could shoot with both feet, and was brave and willing enough to look for goals. His one regret was that Osgood was not on Orient's staff.

His first senior run-out came in a League Cup-tie with Workington in which he scored a goal near the end and was promptly thrust back in the reserves again. That was not surprising for the regular first team leader was international Barry Bridges, so it was one of the not infrequent 'Docherty bombshells' when three days after Bridges had played for England he was dropped to substitute for the League game against Leicester and Osgood entrusted with the leadership of the attack.

No one, least of all Osgood, rated that first outing a success as Chelsea plunged to a 2–0 defeat on their own ground, but

Docherty persevered and soon Osgood was attracting comments from informed critics as easily as a flame draws moths. Ronnie Allen, who was capped five times for England as a centre-forward, said that Osgood travelled as though gliding over water; former Chelsea and international star, Roy Bentley, could not recall a youngster making such an impact in less than six months; Bedford Jezzard, another England leader, said simply that he was the best since Tommy Lawton; and Nat Lofthouse described him as the prototype for the footballer of the future, a man who could play anywhere and do any job. Old-timers compared him with David Jack, and the moderns with Jimmy Greaves and the great Brazilian, Pele, and that he should follow their example by being capped at 18.

In October, 1965, when he was still four months short of his 19th birthday, Osgood was given ten matches in which to establish himself. Long before he had completed them, the pressure on Sir Alf Ramsey to include him in the England squad was building up. On succesive Saturdays he helped to destroy three of the country's leading sides, Spurs, Liverpool and Burnley, scoring in each of them and twice notching the winner.

Against Burnley, Osgood played a midfield linking role throughout the first half, and his goal came when the players should have been relaxing in the dressing room for 49 minutes had passed, the referee explaining later that he added the extra for time-wasting. But the incident that made the game memorable came nine minutes after the break when Osgood received the ball just inside his own half. He dribbled round three challenges, by tremendous acceleration evaded another, and then hammered the ball left-footed past the advancing Adam Blacklaw, the Burnley goalkeeper. It was a solo performance which drew all the partisan fans in the Turf Moor stand to their feet as if magnets had been placed just above their heads. Altogether he had run 60 yards in deep mud and left his rivals stranded like a Derby favourite winning by a distance from a field of handicappers.

By this time, Osgood had a clear conception of the role of a modern centre-forward. In terms of enterprise, he was essentially a leader, and ready to pit his long, lean body against a massed defence. But he also liked the midfield station where he could see the shape of things ahead and where he could develop his rapid eye for spotting the unmarked man.

By this time, Docherty, who had been so cautious when the possibility of Osood becoming an England player was first mentioned, was ecstatic about his protégé's capabilities. He is on record as saying: 'He's the greatest. You can't coach him, and I wouldn't dare to for fear of spoiling his natural ability. I shall leave him to mature like wine. He has the touch of a surgeon. Beyond that, he's brave and loves the game. I let him run free to play by ear.'

As for Osgood, he said that it was easier for him to play in midfield where he could advance and take on opponents from the front than stay up front where he had to turn with the ball, which was not so easy for a man of his build.

Osgood did not, in the end, win a place in the World Cup side which brought the Jules Rimet trophy to England that wonderfully exciting July of 1966 possibly because, after that fantastic goal against Burnley he lost his scoring touch and netted only once in his last 24 first team appearances that season – the header that beat Munich to put Chelsea in the semi-final of the Fairs' Cup. He spent the summer settling down in a new house at Windsor and was told when he reported back at Stamford Bridge that he would be the side's penalty-taker, which, Docherty hoped, would restore his flair for banging them in.

By October Osgood had scored six of the 23 goals which put Chelsea on top of the First Division and then tragedy struck in the 27th minute of a League Cup-tie at Blackpool. Osgood went into a 50-50 challenge with left-back Emlyn Hughes, fell awkwardly and rolled over in agony, his right leg fractured just above the ankle, a complete accident that gave Osgood the sickening fear that he would never again become the potential power that he was, with an under-23 cap against Wales to be picked up in a week's time.

Osgood cracked with a joviality he must have been far from feeling: 'You had better change my name to Wasgood.'

Chelsea splashed out £100,000 on Tony Hateley from Aston Villa to plug the gap while Osgood worked out a programme for his rehabilitation which began with twice-weekly visits to Stamford Bridge for a course of body exercises. Possibly he was too keen, for when doctors examined him in December they decided that his leg would have to remain in thigh-high plaster for another two months, and Chelsea did their best to ease the boredom of his inactivity by taking him to Blackpool while the side prepared for the Cup. Then, just as he threw away his crutches at the end of January, 1967, he contracted tonsillitis!

So it was April before Osgood was back in training, beginning by running up and down the terraces to strengthen his leg muscles, but he missed the Cup Final in which Chelsea went down 2–1 to Spurs and also, much to his annoyance, the club's trip to America. But by July, he was passed as fully fit again, and Chelsea sold the stand-in Hateley to Liverpool.

It could not be expected that Osgood would resume in the same menacing form he had been showing at the time of his injury ten months earlier for now there was more circumspection in his play and he was waiting for someone to kick him on that suspect right foot without causing any damage to restore his confidence. Only three goals came in his first eleven League games before the shock resignation of Docherty followed immediately that October by a 7–0 flop at Leeds. The numbing effect of this defeat was neutralised for Osgood by his call-up for the under-23 team to meet Wales so that the chance denied to him by his injury was now being repeated in the same fixture a year later.

Osgood's international baptism was indeed a watery one for although his career as an England player was only eight minutes old when he scored, torrential rain made the match a farce. As a test of stamina, if any were needed, it served its purpose but the soccer skills were submerged on a pitch of thick mud and surface water. Swansea was aptly named that night as England ploughed to a 2–1 victory.

The rehabilitation of Ossie was not achieved without frequent stumbles and injuries, and illness deprived him of the chance for an advancement that seemed his for the taking. Damage to an ankle cost him a visit to Greece, Bulgaria and Yugoslavia in 1968 and the following summer the weakening effect of the tonsils operation ruled him out of a three match assault on Belgium, Holland and Portugal.

With this discouraging background, it is perhaps not surprising that Osgood turned author and in a depressed state of mind said that he did not think he would ever play for England because he could not build up his work-rate to match his skill. Certainly he was inconsistent and he did not relish the increasing aggression of the game, a militant combativeness caused by the widening gulf between the rewards of success and the price of failure.

Following defeats at Liverpool and West Ham, Chelsea dropped Osgood at the start of the 1969 season when Osgood admitted that he could not cope with the massive demands made on the fitness and mental attitudes of midfield players. But that view changed again at Christmas when Chelsea scored eight goals, including five against Crystal Palace at Selhurst Park, and he scored four of them. It was obvious that someone had been rekindling the fire to go with the flair that made him one of the most talked-about hopes of English football in the last decade.

A hat-trick against Sunderland, snapped up with devastating sharpness, increased the clamour to Sir Alf Ramsey to name him in the England squad, a clamour that was even echoed by a rector in his parish magazine, with critics pointing out that whereas England had scored only twice in three games, Osgood already had 16 beside his name for a season halfway through – a sharp contrast to his meagre nine in the whole of the previous campaign.

Nine more goals, including a Cup hat-trick against Queen's Park Rangers, at last persuaded Sir Alf that the time had come to call up Osgood and the Chelsea star received the news that he had been chosen for the squad to go to Brussels soon after his 23rd birthday.

The conditions for the introduction of Osgood to the full England side bore a depressing similarity to those for his initial representative appearance at Swansea, although this time the elements substituted hail for rain.

Even so, England skilfully mastered the mud and Osgood played his part in making the first goal for Alan Ball in a 3–1 victory. The verdict of the critics was that Osgood, whose own expertise had been drawn out by the highly-developed play of those around him, could book his passage for Mexico and this view was underlined when he scored two goals in an under-23 match against the Scots which a blizzard halted after an hour.

By now, Osgood was very much a front man, far more at home as a striker than as a midfield forager, perferring to provide the threat rather than being the one to be threatened. His flair and appetite for goals had much to do with Chelsea reaching their Wembley final in 1970, but Osgood was far from satisfied with his performance. The match on a pitch like a treacle sponge was not the greatest of soccer spectacles but it was certainly a cliff-hanger with Leeds in front twice and Chelsea gallantly pulling back each time. In a game in which he was largely eclipsed, Osgood's best contribution was to have a shot cleared off the line.

But the replay at Old Trafford the following week provided an ideal example of why Osgood must rank as one of the most exciting and dynamic forwards in present day football. Once again Leeds were in front, thanks to a great goal by Mick Jones, but now it was Osgood who lit the fuse to Chelsea's flagging efforts as he ghosted in from the left to head Charlie Cooke's chip wide of David Harvey for the equaliser. When David Webb put Chelsea ahead, scoring what transpired to be the decisive goal, it was the first time the London side had been in the lead in this titanic struggle which lasted 210 minutes, the first time a replay had been necessary to a Wembley Cup Final.

With 31 goals for the season, Osgood went to Mexico for the World Cup as England's leading scorer but his role there was confined to that of substitute for the matches against Rumania and Czechoslovakia.

If this was something of an anti-climax for him, the trip at least capped a tremendous season in which, apart from his first appearances in a full England side and in the Cup Final, he was ranked third to Billy Bremner, of Leeds, and Stoke goal-keeper, Gordon Banks, by the Football Writers' Association in their ballot for the Player of the Year, and in that position he could claim to be the leading forward.

When the 1970-71 campaign opened, Osgood was made joint favourite with Astle and Royle to top the scoring charts for the season. What of Royle, proud possessor of a championship medal and yet little more than on the threshold of his career? Perhaps the 'great' tag should not be ascribed to him thus early. Yet the critical fans of Goodison Park, reared on the feats of

Dean and Lawton, have already conferred it and the impartial who have watched his progress these last few years have noticed the steady closing of the gap between potential and performance.

For Royle to earn a place among the illustrious creates no precedent, for what of the Busby Babes, those sterling youngsters of Manchester United, and Duncan Edwards in particular? Edwards had only four full seasons in first class soccer before his death as a result of the Munich air crash. But that was long enough for him to win 18 caps. If Edwards was the player of the late fifties, then Royle could equally be so of the early seventies.

And Royle could so easily have gone to Manchester United, for though he was born in Liverpool the Old Trafford men were his favourites. He went to the same school where Beatles John Lennon and Paul McCartney were educated and since he was the son of an accomplished pianist it was not surprising that he took a keen interest in music and enjoyed the pop scene.

An early accident could have put all thoughts of soccer out of Royle's mind for he broke his left leg in a game when he was 13. He came back so well that his headmaster advised the local selectors to have a look at him and, liking what they saw, they included him in the powerful Liverpool Schools' side although honours eluded them during Royle's stay in the team.

What immediately impressed those early observers was Royle's exceptional heading ability, and when he joined Everton in the summer of 1965 the task was to make him as sound on the ground as he was dangerous in the air. He was easy-going, too apt to shrug off failure with a smile rather than a snarl. And although he was big, there was nothing burly about him for he had not fully developed his strength. So right from the outset there was extra training for Joe and, even while his colleagues were enjoying their short summer respite, there was the youngster sweating it out with body-building stints in that vast, empty stadium where the stands seem to echo with every panting breath. His industry not only sharpened his skills but steeled his resolve, and the time soon passed when Royle was a push-over for any defender. As he once remarked, things happen so quickly in the penalty area, the first effort has to count.

Royle was still only a 15-year-old apprentice when he made

his first appearance in Everton's Central League side, and he had scored five goals in 14 games for them when he was pitched into his League debut against Blackpool in January, 1966. It was an awe inspiring task for a youngster. Here he was still three months short of his 17th birthday and ordered to replace the Scottish maestro, Alex Young, against Blackpool. Everton lost 2–0, and Royle, the youngest man to appear in Everton's League side, scarcely caused a quiver of apprehension in the Blackpool defence.

The fans were unanimous in their verdict. Royle should not have played. So for a while he returned to comparative obscurity while Everton nurtured the find they were certain would become a star.

Just eleven days after his 18th birthday he was back in the League side, hitting two goals in a 3–1 victory over Chelsea, yet elation at this break-through was soured by reports that he had punched rather than headed in the first. To score goals apparently was not enough, they had to be seen to be scored – without argument.

Altogether there were four League outings for Royle towards the end of that 1966-67 season which meant when the next campaign opened he was a probable rather than a possible for the team and, in fact, he did so well that by December much of Everton's striking power rested on his shoulders. The skill which was inbred in him was gradually drawn out on one of the toughest of testing grounds. He moved intelligently and swiftly, ever seeking the space and time, albeit only a fleeting moment, to hammer header or shot at the opponents' goal.

Filling the number nine shirt to the satisfaction of the populace on the Goodison Park terraces was no easy task and the fact that Royle did so was a tribute to his industry and talent. That shrewd manager, Harry Catterick, is not one to heap praise on his players but his own assessment of Royle was made plain when he sold England centre-forward, Fred Pickering, to Birmingham, and released Alex Young to become player-manager of the Irish club, Glentoran.

In Everton's run to the Cup Final in 1968, there was no better goal than that achieved by Royle in an incredible individual effort against Carlisle. On a muddy pitch, Royle picked up the ball in his own half and cleaved through the Carlisle defence. He was still being chased by two desperate rivals when he calmly picked his spot and rammed the ball past Alan Ross, giving the goalkeeper no hope of saving, even though he had narrowed the angle as far as he could.

If any soccer event on its own could prove that Royle had arrived, this was it. He could now shoot unhesitatingly with both feet and from any position and his 16 goals in 33 games that season indicated his growing menace. Leicester had been victims of a hat-trick performance – Royle's first since he was 15 – and the game was at Goodison where visiting teams like to play tight. For himself, Royle prefers games away from home where opponents are committed more to an attacking policy rather than on his own pitch where he is confronted by massed defences.

In the summer of 1968, Royle toured the continent with England's under-23's, playing against Hungary in Budapest, and by the time the 1970 season opened he had increased his total of appearances for this side to seven and was so much a fixture that he was an ever-present in Everton's championship-winning team, a proud record he shared with three other colleagues, goalkeeper Gordon West, full-back Tommy Wright and midfield player, John Hurst.

Perhaps it is a sign of the fertility of the Merseyside soccer environment that, apart from West, all three were born in Liverpool and graduated through junior soccer there.

Royle, who lives with his parents in the Norris Green district of Liverpool, walks down the road knowing that he earns five or six times more than other young men of his age there. Quick success has not spoiled him. Naturally he is eager to reach out for the glittering rewards that soccer has to offer but for him the interests of Everton and the game are still paramount. And long may it remain so, for he is one of our great hopes, matured in one of the world's most demanding areas.